# Introduction to Geocaching with the Garmin GPS

## A Treasure Hunting Adventure

www.GeocachingClassroom.com

Copyright © 2010 Paul Scime' All rights reserved. No part of this book may be reproduced in any form, or by any electronic, mechanical, or other means, without permission in writing from the publisher.

ISBN-13: 978-0-9820631-1-8     ISBN-10: 0-9820631-1-3

Publication Data
Scime', Paul.
Geocaching with a Garmin GPS A family Treasure hunting Adventure.
    Includes index
    ISBN 0-9820631-1-3
    1. Hiking & Camping   2. Outdoor Recreation
    I. Title

The publisher and the author make no representation or warranties with respect to the accuracy or completeness of the contents of this work and specifically disclaim all warranties, including without limitation warranties of fitness for a particular purpose. The advice and strategies contained herein may not be suitable for every situation. This work is sold with the understanding that the publisher is not engaged in rendering legal, accounting, or other professional services. The fact that an organization or website is referred to in this work as a citation and or potential source of further information does not mean that the author or publisher endorses the information the organization or website may provide or recommendations it may make. Further readers should be aware that Internet websites listed in this work may have changed or disappeared between when this work was written and when it is read.

Neither the author nor publisher shall have any liability to any person of entity with respect to any loss or damage caused or alleged to be caused directly or indirectly by the instructions contained in this book or by any software and hardware products described in it.

Product names and websites mentioned in this book are trademarks of their perspective companies. Garmin is a trademark of Garmin, LTD. Google Earth™ mapping service is a trademark of Google, Inc. Geocaching.com is a trademark of Groundspeak, Inc. No such use of any trade name is intended to convey endorsement or other affiliation with this book. This book is not endorsed or affiliated with Garmin, inc., Groundspeak, Inc. or Google, Inc. or any other manufacturer or publisher mentioned in this book.

This book is available at a special discount when purchased in bulk for premium and sales promotions as well as fund raising and educational use. For information contact the publisher: Prime Technology Corporation, P.O. Box 784501, Winter Garden, Florida 34778

 *www.GeocachingClassroom.com*

## About the Author

**Paul Scime'** has been a high school teacher for over twenty years in Orlando, Florida. He has previously authored software and texts on a variety of subjects including Digital Electronics, Fiber Optics, Applied Mathematics, and living a frugal lifestyle in *"The Frugal Factor."*

Paul first discovered geocaching while searching the Internet for a good deal on computer hardware. Peaked by his curiosity, his search for computer hardware took a completely different turn into the world of geocaching. He was intrigued by the fact that there were geocaches hidden all over the world, including several in his own neighborhood. This led to the purchase of his first GPS, and the start of many family adventures to hunt for geocaches.

Since that time he has explained geocaching to family and friends throughout the country, and has integrated geocaching into his high school curriculum.

Code 12931

# Acknowledgements

This book could not have been completed without the amazing support people at both Garmin Ltd., and Geocaching.com. The resources they provided and fast answers to my e-mail's kept this book on track.

To all my high school students who have solved hundreds of puzzles throughout the years, leading them to virtual caches on the school campus. Their interest has provided the motivation to find additional ways to integrate geocaching with education.

Finally, a special thanks to my family who have put up with my many geocaching adventures, and my obsession for technical gadgets.

The adventure continues, as there is always another cache to find!

# Contents

**Chapter 1** **Geocaching** 7
Introduction to Geocaching 7
Why Geocache 10
Geocaching Steps 13
Types of Caches 14
Starting Your Journey 15
Naked Geocaching 17
Ready Set Go 19
Finding a Cache 21
Signature Items 23
Beware of the Mugglers! 24
Logging Your Find 24
Travel Bugs, Geocoins, and Geotokens 25
Finding Benchmarks 27

**Chapter 2** **How the GPS System Works** 29

**Chapter 3** **Placing your own Cache** 31
Choosing a Location 31
Cache Containers 32
Cache Contents 33
Submitting a Cache 34

**Chapter 4** **Purchasing a GPS** 35

**Chapter 5** **Geocaching Terms** 39

**Chapter 6** **Understanding the Garmin GPS** 47
Software Updates 47
Garmin GPS Functions 48
Turning It On 48
Compass Page 49
Main Menu 50
Map Page 50
Power/Backlight Key 51
Quit Key 51

*Geocaching with a Garmin GPS*

| | |
|---|---|
| Zoom in/out | 51 |
| Find Key | 52 |
| Enter/Rocker Key | 54 |
| Satellite Page | 54 |
| WAAS | 55 |
| Marking a Waypoint | 57 |
| Hiding Caches | 58 |
| Finding a Waypoint/Geocache | 59 |
| Manually Entering Geocaches | 61 |
| Deleting Waypoints/Geocaches | 62 |
| Tracks | 63 |
| Recent Finds | 65 |

| | | |
|---|---|---|
| **Chapter 7** | **Setting up for Geocaching** | **67** |
| | Set Up | 67 |
| | System | 68 |
| | Display | 68 |
| | Page Sequence | 69 |
| | Map | 70 |
| | Geocache | 71 |
| | Units | 71 |
| | Welcome Message | 72 |
| | Trip Computer | 73 |

| | | |
|---|---|---|
| **Chapter 8** | **Geocaching with the Garmin GPS** | **75** |
| | Managing Geocaching Files | 75 |
| | Transferring GPS Files | 77 |
| | Loading Caches from Geocaching.com | 78 |
| | Transferring Saved Files | 78 |
| | Viewing Caches with Google Earth | 79 |

| | | |
|---|---|---|
| **Chapter 9** | **Geocaching Links** | **85** |
| | **Index** | **87** |
| | **Resources** | **90** |
| | Hidden Cache Logs | 90 |
| | Found Cache Logs | 96 |

 *www.GeocachingClassroom.com*

# Chapter 1
# Geocaching

## INTRODUCTION TO GEOCACHING

We parked the van just a few miles from our home. Quickly I heard, "Can we go?" I glanced back and barely got out, when the doors flew open, as my family was on the hunt for our latest cache find.

As I watched the kids running, generally in the same direction, I ran after them glancing down at the GPS. The numbers dropped. I moved faster, sometimes running behind, ahead, and to the side of my children. I followed a trail as it wound between trees, and finally into a small clearing. I watched as the GPS receiver showed 318 feet.......212....85....8... Finally, the family merged in the same area. We swarmed like insects looking for the cache. I paid too much attention to my GPS trying to find the exact cache location (otherwise known as ground zero) when my daughter yelled, "I found it!"

The geocache was a military ammo box hidden in the hollow of a tree. Opening it, we found many items, including a deck of cards, kids meal toys, a porcelain thimble, a softball, two travel bugs and a geocoin. The kids decided to trade the softball for a toy top. After the trade we signed the log, left our signature geotoken and put everything back just as we found it.

We were so engaged with the hunt, we did not realize what was around us. As we turned to begin our walk back to the van we looked up to see a beautiful lake. On our return walk we saw two blue herons near the lake, and a few armadillos wandering the woods. Finding the geocache was fun and the kids enjoyed their trade, but the real treasure was the journey.

The activity described above is called geocaching. Geocaching is a modern day, high tech activity looking for treasure in the form of inexpensive trade items that others have hidden. It is a challenging adventure that can be a safe and fulfilling activity for people of all ages and abilities. Geocaching is a simple concept. Someone hides a collection of items, such as small toys and trinkets in a waterproof container called a cache. The cache also contains a logbook. When found each person signs the log, and trades something for one of the items in the cache. When the cache is hidden, the location of the cache is carefully recorded using a GPS receiver, and then the location and description are posted on a website. That's when the hunt begins.

In just a few years, geocaching has grown incredibly popular. It is an excellent family activity. It uses technology, but you don't need to be a technology nerd to do it. The learning curve is very small. By the end of reading this you will be able to go out and find your first geocache.

### So, just what is a Geocacher?
A geocacher or cacher is a person who is looking for one of thousands of caches (hidden treasure) planted by fellow players. Today there are over 1,138,124 caches hidden in 200 countries. Geocaches are everywhere. The fact is that you probably pass several every day.

### What Is a Geocache?
A geocache pronounced /GEE-oh-cash/ is a hidden container of trade items. Typically, a geocache is an ammo box, Tupperware type container, or even an old peanut butter jar. Inside you will find a logbook, and other small items like key chains, kids meal toys, Frisbees, etc. The explorer who finds the box signs the logbook, swaps an item and leaves the box in its original location.

When hidden, the exact GPS coordinates are taken using a handheld GPS receiver. The person who hides the cache logs

  *www.GeocachingClassroom.com*

the coordinates on one of many web sites devoted to geocaching.

When you visit these web sites you can type in your zip code to locate caches in your area. The list of caches will include the GPS coordinates, logs from cachers who have already found the cache, and more. Load these coordinates in your GPS and off you go looking for the hidden treasure!

A cache is typically well hidden so that people who are not actually looking for it don't find it by mistake. The sight of people walking around a park in circles staring at what looks like a cell phone can be strange to those who do not know about geocaching. These people who are not in the know are called mugglers. (Yes, this term was taken from the Harry Potter novels) Mugglers do not understand the sport and may move, steal or damage the cache.

## Beware of the mugglers!

# Why Geocache?

From the start, geocaching appealed to those who enjoy playing with technology. Today people from all walks of life, ages and physical abilities enjoy geocaching. Below are a few of the many reasons to start geocaching.

**Family Activity** – geocaching is an excellent family activity. Everyone can participate, from selecting caches to look for, to actually finding the caches. Geocaching can be a wonderful family adventure. My children enjoy looking for the larger caches. Finding just one cache on a trip is never enough, so we often plan out several caches to find. The kids like taking turns swapping trade items.

**Exercise** – Geocaching can be a low or high impact workout. It just depends on the caches you select. Many caches are simply "Park and Grabs," which means you can park within a few feet of the cache. Others may require a long hike or climb. So if you need an interesting way to get a little exercise, geocaching may be the perfect activity. It's much cheaper than a gym membership!

**Wonderful Distraction** – We all get caught in a rut sometimes. Geocaching gives you something different to do with friends and family, or even alone.

Any time we plan a long vacation, I use Google Earth to look at our route and download caches to my GPS. (Later I will show you how to locate geocaches using Google Earth.) I don't usually stop for all the caches, but when I get tired of driving, getting out of the car to look for a cache gives me a chance to stretch my legs. Geocaching is a great way to break up the monotony of a long journey.

**Business Trips** – Stuck in a hotel away from home? Go geocaching instead of watching TV! Many geocaches are placed near convention centers, hotels, and large corporate headquarters. If you travel for business, geocaching can give you something to do in that down time. It's also a great stress reliever. Geocaching is also used by many businesses as team building exercises. (See www.GeocachingClassroom.com for more information on team building.)

**Brain Games** – Don't just exercise your body. Exercise your mind, too! Getting out to new places and new experiences is good for the mind and body. Some caches require solving puzzles and clues. These caching clues will lead you from one cache to another. These are called multicaches.

## *It's the journey, not the prize!*

What's in the container doesn't really matter. The ultimate prize is the journey itself. Geocaching can be one of the best tour guides you will ever have. It can lead you to beautiful and interesting places you never knew existed. Often those places are in your own hometown!

A hand held GPS will get you within 20 feet of the cache. After that you need to start looking under logs, bushes, in trees and around lampposts. There is no end to the creativity of the people who hide caches.

Some caches are easy to find, commonly called Park and Grabs (PnG) but some are more challenging, requiring a three mile walk in a nature preserve, or hidden on a cliff requiring climbing gear. But rest assured that there are caches hidden for all capabilities.

There is even a site dedicated to geocaching for those with physical disabilities (see the geocaching links section). When a cache is listed, the cache hider will list the requirements and ease of getting to the cache. So you will know what you're getting into before you leave the house! Some caches even require a boat and diving gear!

# GEOCACHING STEPS

- Find caches on the internet
- Print cache information
- Load caches into your GPS
- Search and find caches
- Sign the log
- Take something and leave something
- Log your find

### Who Geocaches?

People from all walks of life are geocaching: doctors, lawyers, teachers, car mechanics, bikers, supermarket grocery clerks, even your dentist may be a geocacher. There are geocaches hidden for all ages and abilities. If you like scavenger hunts, spy movies, puzzle solving, and treasure maps you will like geocaching.

*Geocaching with a Garmin GPS*

## TYPES OF CACHES

**Traditional** - This is the original cache consisting of a waterproof container and a logbook. Normally the container is a Tupperware container or ammo box filled with goodies.

**Micro Cache** - This cache is very small. (The size of a 35mm film container or smaller.) It usually only contains a logbook.

**Multi-Cache** - This type of cache involves more that one location. There will be several caches; the first one might contain the coordinates to the next cache, or a puzzle that must be solved to figure out the next coordinates. The second cache leads to the third cache and so on...

**Virtual Cache** – This type of cache does not contain a physical box. A virtual cache is just a location. To claim that you have found the location you would need to log the coordinates or be able to answer questions about the location.

**Webcam Cache** - This type of cache is at the location of an Internet web camera. The idea is to visit the location and get yourself on camera. The difficulty here is that you would need to call a friend to look up the webcam address to see if the camera shows you and record a screenshot.

**Puzzle Cache** - This cache involves solving several complicated puzzles to find the coordinates of the next cache.

**EarthCache** –These caches are places of special geoscientific significance; an area that displays the unique features of the Earth and how geological forces have formed it. Examples include rock formations, hot springs, craters and canyons. See EarthCache.org for more information.

**Event Cache** – An event cache is a cache that is part of a local meeting of state or regional caching clubs. Families often attend these events, and they usually take place in kid friendly areas such as parks, and recreational areas. These clubs designate special caches and a time and place to meet. Usually after the event these caches are archived.

 *www.GeocachingClassroom.com*

# STARTING YOUR JOURNEY

Geocaching requires the stealth of James Bond, the adventurous spirit of Indiana Jones, and the deductive reasoning of Sherlock Holmes. But to get started geocaching all you need is Internet access and the will to explore!

Your first step is to find the caches in your area. Go to a geocaching site such as Geocaching.com and search for local caches. When at Geocaching.com click on *Hide and Seek a Cache*. This will bring you to a page that will allow you to look for caches in a variety of ways. Note: a GC code is a unique code given to every geocache on geocaching.com.

Search by:

- ✓ **Address**
- ✓ **Postal Code**
- ✓ **State**
- ✓ **Country**
- ✓ **Longitude and Latitude**
- ✓ **GC code**

*Geocaching with a Garmin GPS*

The cache size and difficulty are listed on the site. When caching with my children, I usually search for large caches. They enjoy taking turns trading items with the caches. But, they also like searching for micro caches near Wal-Mart, Cracker Barrel and other restaurants!

Size: ■ (Regular)

Difficulty: ★★☆☆☆

(1 is easiest, 5 is hardest)

Terrain: ★★☆☆☆

## Premium Member Benefits

A premium membership on Geocaching.com provides additional features including:
- Organize geocache listings and create favorite lists with the bookmark feature.
- Create custom searches based on cache size, location and more with pocket queries.
- Receive instant notification about newly published caches.
- Search geocaches along a route.
- Increase your Google earth views from 25 to 250.
- Access to premium member only caches.

Currently the premium membership cost is $30 annually.

www.GeocachingClassroom.com

# NAKED GEOCACHING

If you don't have a GPS, start out by "Naked Geocaching." Naked geocaching is a term that simply means geocaching without the use of a GPS device. Here's how you can cache naked:

1. Go to Geocaching.com and enter your zip code. This will show you all the caches near your location. Note: you will need an account in order to see the cache coordinates. So, sign up for a basic account. It's FREE.

2. Select a large cache that's in an area that you are familiar with. The size of the cache is shown in the graphic of four squares. The larger the colored squares, the larger the size of the cache container.

3. After you have signed into your account you will be able to see the cache coordinates. Also, on the left hand side of the screen are two maps. Scroll down to see the map on the lower part of the page. At the top of the map click, "View Larger Map."

4. When the large map page appears, click on, "Satellite." Now you will see the satellite picture along with all the street names. Zoom in as far as you can to get an accurate idea of the cache location.

Note: the location of the cache on the map is not exact. Only attempt to find large caches using this method.

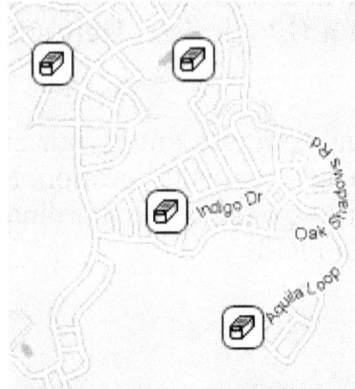

5. At this point you can jump into your car and start looking for your first cache. Don't forget to print the map and cache page before you leave. Reading the hints and cache logs may give you clues to the cache's location.

6. You can also see nearby caches on the map. To view the full caching information page click on the icon, then on the cache name.

That system will work for your first few large cache finds. It will get you close to the cache, but by using that method, you may not get close enough to some caches. The next step is to purchase a GPS unit. Visit GeocachingClassroom.com for up to date reviews of the newest GPS units.

If you already have a GPS, download the locations to your GPS. (See the GPS tutorial for information on downloading.) Select a few caches. Usually there is more than one cache in an area. Load up several caches in the area, that way if you're close to another one; you can increase your daily cache count.

www.GeocachingClassroom.com

# READY, SET, GO

Now, round up the family and friends, get in the car and go. It really requires at least two people when caching. It's difficult to look at a hand held GPS and drive safely. When starting your journey be sure to bring a flashlight, a calculator, a camera (for recording the event), and something small to leave in the cache. Some caches will include mathematical puzzles, which will lead you to another cache. Usually the math is simple, but it's always good to have a calculator handy.

### *What to bring:*
- Printed cache page
- Cell phone
- Water
- Flashlight
- First aid kit
- Insect repellant
- Pen and pencil
- Camera
- Extra batteries
- Sunglasses
- Proper clothing
- Trade items

When I first started geocaching we were on a 1200-mile trip that took us through West Virginia. I had downloaded several caches to my GPS. One of the caches was Simpson Creek Covered Bridge GCQNHM. It sounded interesting so I made a point of stopping for that cache. Unfortunately, when we arrived it was dark. The cache was in the covered bridge and after 20 minutes of searching in the dark, I gave up. On our way back home from our vacation I returned to the covered bridge. This time I made sure I had a flashlight and once again we arrived in the dark – but this time, with my dollar store flashlight, I was able to find the cache.

If the cache is in the woods or on a nature trail be sure to use your GPS to mark the car's location before you begin your search. One of the last things you want is to find that cache, and not be able to find the car! (See Marking Waypoints and Tracks)

Think of how many times you have walked out of the supermarket or mall and forgot where you parked your car!

## Drunken Bee Dance

Bees actually communicate with each other about food sources using dances. But in this case the drunken bee is the geocacher. The dance is the movement of a geocacher, trying to pinpoint Ground Zero. The geocacher chases the directional arrow first in one direction, and then in another in an attempt to locate the hidden cache.

## FINDING A CACHE

Park as close to the coordinates as you can and then you are off by foot. Your GPS will get you within 20 feet or closer. After that you will need to use your geosenses to find the cache. Some caches are large like ammo boxes. Others are very small or micro caches the size of 35 MM film canisters, or smaller!

Be conspicuous as you are hunting for the cache. You don't want to give the location away to the general public. Pretend you're in a spy movie. Use great stealth to retrieve the cache. You may need to pretend your GPS is a cell phone or camera so you don't give away your true mission!

Many micro caches are magnetic and may be hidden on the sides, top or bottom of any metal object. I found a magnetic cache on a stop sign that was painted the exact same shade as the stop sign. It was so small that I almost missed it. Looking from the side, it made the stop sign look like it had a large red pimple.

When you find a cache, sign the logbook. Logbooks vary in size from small strips of paper carefully rolled up to fit in a micro cache, to full size notebooks. When signing the logbook,

*Geocaching with a Garmin GPS*

put down your cache handle (the name you use on the cache web site), the time, date, and what state or country you're from. This information makes it interesting for the next cacher. I have been to caches that were visited less than an hour before I arrived!

Some cache sites are very popular. If you visit tourist areas like Orlando, Florida or Las Vegas, Nevada you will find caches that have been visited by people from around the world. Reading the log books at these cache sites can be very interesting.

As you search through the cache box, take one item from the cache and leave your item. Remember most caches do not contain anything of real value. Usually kids meal toys, key chains, and such. You don't have to leave anything in the cache; you can just sign the log. If you take something out of the cache you should then leave a trade item of equal or greater value.

Do not place improper items in the cache. Never place food inside a cache container. Food would attract insects and animals. Also, never place anything dangerous in a cache such as knives, fireworks or alcohol. Remember that geocaching is a family friendly activity.

## Business Caches

If you know the longitude and latitude, you can search for nearby caches. So, if you are planning a vacation or business trip, look at the hotel's website for the GPS coordinates. Many hotels and businesses list their longitude and latitude coordinates on their websites, or you can use www.GPSvisualizer.com to convert postal addresses to longitude and latitude coordinates.

## SIGNATURE ITEMS

Leave a signature item if you have one. A signature item is an item that a geocacher leaves in a cache that is uniquely theirs. It's a cacher's way of making his or her mark on a newly found cache. Signature items are often business cards with the cachers geocaching name, the city, state or town that they are from, and a logo or picture of the cachers. A signature item can be anything that is unique to the cacher that they leave in each cache. Georace.net sells geotoken kits that allow you to design custom geotokens with your geocaching name, and logo. After you have made the transaction, carefully put the cache back exactly where you found it!

## Beware of the Mugglers!

When finding a cache, be aware of the people around you. Most people do not have knowledge of the activity and may damage, move, or steal the cache. The term for these people is muggler. Cachers refer to non-cachers as mugglers, a term from the Harry Potter novels by J.K. Rowling. In the novels a muggle is a person that isn't a wizard or witch, or doesn't have magical powers.

A muggler may discover a cache after seeing a cacher discover it. When a muggler discovers a cache it is likely to become lost or stolen. Caches placed in busy areas often come with the warning, "Beware of the mugglers."

## Logging Your Find

When you get back to your computer go to the site where the cache was listed and log your find. In the log, list what you took, what was left behind, the condition of the cache, and update what travel bugs were actually in the cache. If the cache contains water or needs some repair, the person who placed the cache will be notified. Also, the next person visiting the cache may bring supplies to make the repair. So far, the caching community has been very respectful in keeping the caches in good condition.

If you found the cache container unique and the hide challenging, thank the cache hider in your log. The person who placed the cache will receive an email of your log. If you leave information in the log that might give away the location of the cache be sure to encrypt that part of your log. Encrypting a log is done automatically by selecting a check box.

## TRAVEL BUGS AND GEOCOINS

Travel bugs and geocoins are items designed to travel from one cache to another. Geocachers can purchase these trackable coins, or travel bugs (they look like dog tags). Each travel bug has a unique serial number. The serial number is trackable. Traditionally the person purchasing the token will give it an objective. The objective could be to visit all 50 states or visit certain countries before returning to its starting location. I have seen tokens that want to spend the winter in Florida and summers in New York.

When you find a token, coin or travel bug, read its objective, If you can help it along its way, take it and log it on the tracking web site. There are many sites that offer trackable items. The purchaser will be watching its travels. So, don't take the trackable token unless you can help it on its journey, and don't hang on to it for too long.

*Geocaching with a Garmin GPS*

Each travel bug has a page on the Geocaching.com website where you can post information and pictures describing the travel bug's journey.

On our vacation to the Grand Canyon area, we deposited five travel bugs, each in a different cache. The objective for each of the travel bugs was to return to a cache near our home. One travel bug made in home in less that three months. This was a journey of over 2,000 miles, made by geocachers simply helping the travel bug on its journey. Another arrived six months later. The other two are still traveling, and one was never heard from.

## TRAVEL BUG PRISON

A Travel Bug Hotel is a cache that requires that you leave as many Travel Bugs as you take. They are called prisons (or jails) because Travel Bugs can get "stuck" in them for an extended period of time. Sometimes people who find the cache don't move any of the Bugs because they didn't have a Bug to leave.

## Finding Benchmarks

A benchmark is a point of reference from which other measurements are taken.

In 1807 President Thomas Jefferson established the United States Coastal Survey (USCS). This government agency became the United States Geological Survey (USGS) and has the task of mapping and surveying the land. Since that time the USGS has placed hundreds of thousands of benchmarks.

These are permanent markers installed by the government to serve as known locations for surveyors and mapmakers. Usually made of brass or aluminum disks, each benchmark is marked with the date it was installed.

Searching for benchmarks is easy because they are not hidden. But be aware some are difficult to get to. However, they are permanent markers in stone or concrete, so you know they have not been muggled.

Because these benchmarks were installed before GPS technology existed, the directions are written for them to be found without a GPS. So, your GPS will get you to the right area, but you will need to rely on the benchmarks written location description to find it.

Note: vegetation may cover the benchmark. It may be on private land. Some are located on highways and busy roads, others in the middle of nowhere. Many have been placed over 100 years ago.

To find benchmarks near you, visit:

www.NGS.NOAA.GOV or www.Geocaching.com

*Geocaching with a Garmin GPS*

# Chapter 2
# How the GPS System Works

This new sport is only possible due to decades of research and over 12 billion dollars worth of satellite hardware orbiting the Earth. These satellites, originally designed for military operations, are helping people find geocaches everyday.

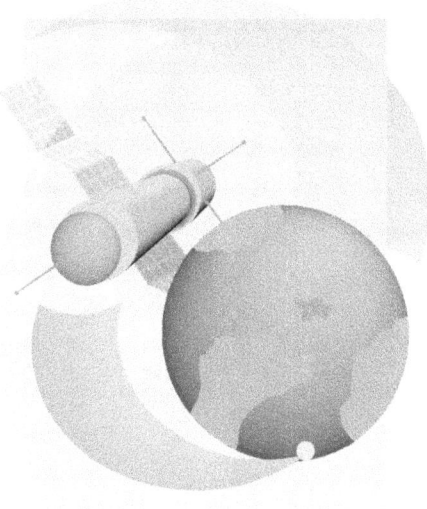

The Global Positioning System (GPS) is the only system that will show you your exact position on earth. This system uses 24 satellites, orbiting the Earth in 6 planes. These satellites orbit 11,000 - 12,000 nautical miles above earth.

The first GPS satellite was launched in 1978. The launch of the 24th satellite in 1994 completed the primary system. These satellites travel at about 7,000 miles per hour, allowing them to circle the Earth in 12 hours. Powered by solar cells, each satellite has an expected life span of 10 years. In 2010 there were 30 satellites dedicated to the GPS network.

These satellites are continuously monitored by five ground stations all around the world, with the main station at Schreiver Air Force Base in Colorado.

The satellites are equipped with an atomic clock, which allows them to transmit signals precisely synchronized with the other satellites. The GPS receiver calculates the time it takes for the signals to travel from the satellite to the GPS receiver. The GPS receiver measures this time from 3 or more satellites and calculates its location, with an accuracy of about 20 feet (6 meters). This technology has brought us a long way from navigating with the stars. These satellites are like modern lighthouses in the sky!

GPS can be used everywhere: land, sea, and air. Since the GPS radio signal is a line of site signal, it will travel through light cloud cover, but will not go through solid objects. So, your hand held GPS will not work in buildings, underwater, in parking garages, or caves... You get the idea.

GPS accuracy was improved with WAAS. WAAS stands for Wide Area Augmentation System. This refers to a network of 25 ground reference stations that cover the entire US, and some parts of Canada and Mexico. Implemented by the FAA (Federal Aviation Administration) for aviation users, these stations send a correction signal to the WAAS satellite. This correction message increases the accuracy of WAAS capable receivers from 10-16 feet (3-5 meters).

 *www.GeocachingClassroom.com*

# Chapter 3
# Placing Your Own Cache

After you have found a few caches, the next step is to hide your own. Placing a cache can be as much fun as finding them! After you place a cache you will get an e-mail each time it is found, listing the comments that were logged by the cacher. It's interesting to see how many people have found your caches and how far they have traveled.

## CHOOSING A LOCATION

When placing your cache, be sure to place it on public property or get permission from the landowner. I have seen caches placed on church property with the permission of the pastor. In that cache we found common trade items and two Bibles! Placing caches on lands administered by the National Parks Service is illegal. Placing a cache on a postal box, or US Post Office Property is also illegal. Remember caches are not to be buried and should not require any digging.

### *Caching Prohibited*
**U.S. Postal property**
**National Parks**
**U.S. Fish & Wildlife areas**
**Near railroad tracks**
**Near military installations**
**Schools**
**Airports**
**Under Bridges**

Think before placing caches. Don't places caches in areas that may be considered a threat to public safety. For example, depending on the location, placing a large cache under a bridge may be considered threatening. It's a good idea to place a label on the outside of the cache stating that it is a

*Geocaching with a Garmin GPS*

geocache. It is also common to place a note inside the cache explaining that geocaching is a global game of hide and seek.

The last thing you want to see is your cache on the news being blown up by the police because they thought it was a bomb.

When you place your cache, be sure your GPS has at least four satellite signals. This will provide an accurate fix of your location. Using the GPS, mark the location, so you have the exact coordinates. (See Marking a Waypoint)

## Cache Containers

It is important to select a quality, waterproof, caching container. 35mm film canisters and Altiod tins are often used but poor choices. They are not truly water tight, resulting in soggy logbooks. Some better choices include:

- **Military ammo boxes**
- **Water proof match containers**
- **Peanut butter jars**
- **Aluminum pill containers**
- **Lock and lock storage containers**

*www.GeocachingClassroom.com*

Geocachers are very creative in designing cache containers. Some are painted with camouflage paint or tape. Others may glue tree bark, grass, rocks or moss on the container so that it blends in with the surrounding environment.

Cachers will also use hollowed out logs, fake sprinkler heads, modified fence post caps and even fake dog poop as ways to hide geocaches.

## Cache Contents

Be sure to place a logbook in the cache. Put a pen or pencil in the cache with the logbook. FREE printable logbooks are available at GeocachingClassroom.com

It's always a good idea to put the logbook in a plastic ziplock bag for added waterproofing. Don't forget to start the cache out with items like key chains and other trinkets for trade.

It is also a common practice to leave a special prize for the first person that finds the cache. Common "First to Find" (FTF) prizes include:

- **Collectible geocoins**
- **Custom FTF geotokens**
- **New travel bugs**
- **Scratch off lottery tickets**
- **Gift cards**

You decide what to leave as a First to Find prize. Anything from custom geotokens, lottery tickets, to gift cards for stores near the cache are good First to Find prizes. Web-sites like Georace.net offer custom First to Find, and geotoken token kits.

Being first to find a cache is a rather prestigious honor. Cachers can sign up to have a weekly email sent from Geocaching .com listing new caches near their home! If you want to be first to a new cache be sure to sign up for this email list.

## SUBMITTING A CACHE

Once you have hidden your cache it must be submitted to Geocaching.com. This is a simple process of filling out a submission form. After the Cache has been reviewed it will be listed on the web site.

Reviewers will look at the location of the cache to make sure it is not in a restricted environment. If the cache is near an environmentally fragile area, too dangerous for cachers, or in restricted areas such as national parks it will not be listed. Visit Geocaching.com for a list of guidelines before hiding your first geocache.

## Chapter 4
# Purchasing a GPS

There are several things to look for when purchasing a new GPS. These include:
- Battery life
- Battery type
- Screen size
- Number of waypoints
- Expandable memory
- Paperless geocaching
- Available maps
- Weight
- Cost

**Battery type** - You will want a GPS that takes readily available batteries. We are talking about AA or AAA batteries. The last thing you want is to have the batteries die when you're out for a day of caching. AA batteries are easily found at convenience stores. Some GPS systems use proprietary rechargeable batteries. If you purchase a GPS that takes a rechargeable battery be sure to also buy a car charger.

**Battery life** - Look for a system with a long battery life. Most have a 12 hour or longer battery life. As with all electronic devices, your battery life will depend on the features used. Using the back light feature will greatly reduce the battery life.

**Screen size and color** - Newer GPS systems have color screens. The color screen is much easier to read. Of course a larger screen is also a bonus.

**Size and weight** - Most hand held units are lightweight. When choosing a GPS for geocaching it is good to find a small handheld unit so that mugglers think you are just looking at you cell phone.

**WAAS** - Today almost all GPS units are WAAS capable. The Wide Area Augmentation System was developed by the FAA to improve the accuracy of the GPS system for aviation.

**Price** - Of course this almost goes without mention. But be careful because some low priced units do not include the interface cable to hook up to your computer. That means you will need to purchase it later. For that additional cost you might want to spend a little more and get a turnkey package. Proprietary cables can cost $50 or more. Today most GPS units use standard micro USB cables.

**Software** - Most companies offer software maps for the US. If you expect to travel to other countries, investigate the cost of maps available for the GPS system you expect to purchase. All the major manufacturers use their own proprietary formats for maps. Mapping software purchased for one brand cannot be used for GPS units made by another manufacturer.

**Memory** - If you only expect to be geocaching memory is not primary concern. Most units have 6 or more megabytes of RAM. Newer units use removable secure digital and micro secure digital flash cards to expand memory.

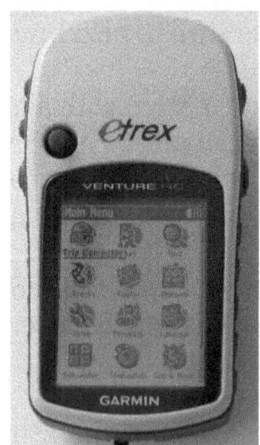

**Geocaches/Waypoints** – Current GPS units will allow you to record or load 500 or more geocache locations. This is adequate since you can also remove them from your GPS and store these locations on your computer.

**Driving Directions** - A GPS with auto routing capability is similar to automotive GPS systems. These units will give you turn by turn driving directions leading you to the cache. This also makes the GPS useful on long car trips.

**Paperless Geocaching** – Newer GPS units allow for paperless geocaching. With paperless geocaching, you have cache descriptions, ratings, and recent log info stored directly on your GPS. So there is no need to take paper printouts along with you.

---

### Dipping

For geocachers, dipping has nothing to do with chewing tobacco. Dipping is the act of logging a travel bug or geocoin into a cache, and immediately logging it back into your possession. Some people use a Travel Bug to track their miles between caches, and will "dip" the travel bug into each cache they find.

---

*Geocaching with a Garmin GPS*

## Chapter 5
# Geocaching Terms

This is a list of geocaching terms and the abbreviations used in logs.

**ALR** – Additional Logging Requirements. The additional steps that must be met before claiming the cache as a find. The owner of the cache reserves the right to delete logs that do not meet the requirement. A common requirement is to email a picture of you at or near the cache find.

**Archived** - A cache that no longer exists, needs maintenance, or has been stolen. These no longer appear when using the search function on geocaching.com.

**ATCF** – As the Crow Flies. Point to point mileage.

**Attribute** – These are the icons on a cache detail page that provide information about a cache. For example: wheel chair accessible, available 24 hours, kid friendly, parking available, restrooms nearby, etc.

**Benchmark** - Geographic marker placed by the US Geological Survey at an exact set of coordinates. Uses benchmarks in a manner similar to virtual caches.

**Bison Tube** – A small metal watertight container that is often used for micro caches, commonly used to hold pills.

**Breeder Cache** – This is a cache that contains free caching containers. The objective is to promote the placement of additional caches. Often it is requested that the cacher note where the caching container came from in the name of the new cache, or in its description.

**BYOP** – Bring your own pen.

**Cache Rating** - Description given on cache pages to help cachers determine the difficulty of caches.

**Cache Machine** – When a group of cachers are out for the purpose of finding as many caches as possible in the shortest period of time.

**CITO** - Cache In, Trash Out. Refers to an ethic whereby cachers leave an area in better shape than they found it by picking up any trash they encounter after finding a cache.

**Datum** – A datum is a standard used for calculating and measuring the longitude and latitude for a given location. Geocaching uses the WGS84 datum.

**Dipping** – The act of logging a travel bug or geocoin into a cache and then immediately logging it back into your possession. Cachers sometimes do this to register miles traveled, before handing the cache off to someone else. Some cachers use a travel bug to track their personal miles traveled between caches.

**DNF** - Did Not Find. Indicates that the cacher searched for a cache, but could not find it.

**Drunken Bee Dance** - The movement of cachers attempting to find ground zero, chasing the direction of their GPS arrow back and forth when near the cache.

**D/T** – This designates the geocaching rating for difficulty and terrain. 1 indicates easiest, 5 is the most difficult.

**EarthCache** – Is a unique cache of geological significance. An earth cache is an area that shows how the planet has been shaped by geological forces.

**Event Cache** – A get together of geocachers, usually to find as many caches in a day and exchange stories about their cache adventures.

www.GeocachingClassroom.com

**Find Score** – Total number of caches found.

**Fire Tacks** – Reflective tacks that are often used to mark trails for night caches.

**FTF** - First to Find. It's very prestigious to be the first to find a cache.

**FTF Token** - A coin or token placed in a cache as a prize for the first cacher that locates the cache.

**GC Code** – The unique identifier associated with every geocache.

**Geocache Series** – A collection of several caches with a common theme.

**Geocoin** - Custom minted coins designed for geocaches. Some coins are trackable.

**Geotoken** – A custom token designed to place in geocaches. Geotokens are not trackable but very collectable. Geotokens are commonly used as first to find prizes and signature items.

**Geotrail** – A worn path that leads directly to the cache.

**GoogleCaching** – Type of virtual geocaching using Google Earth.

**GPSr** - Global Positioning System receiver. Usually referred to just as GPS.

**Ground Zero** - The point at which your GPS claims you should find the cache. When your GPS shows zero feet from the cache location.

**Guard Rail Cache (GRC)** - A cache hidden on or near a highway guardrail.

*Geocaching with a Garmin GPS*

**Hitchhiker** - An object that moves from cache to cache. Eg. travel bugs, geocoins.

**Hydro Cache** – A cache requiring a boat or swimming to retrieve.

**IPV** – In plain view.

**Letterboxing** – Similar to geocaching, whereby using a series of clues, you would find the container, a letterbox. Inside the container is a stamp used to stamp your personal logbook.

**LampPost Cache (LPC)** – A cache hidden near a lamppost. A common and easily found cache.

**Micro** - A very small cache container. Altoids tins, 35MM film canisters and waterproof match holders are common micro containers.

**MKH** – Magnetic key holder. The magnetic hide-a-key often used for micro caches.

**Muggled** – A cache that has been interfered with, or taken by a non-cacher.

**Mugglers** - People encountered that do not know what geocaching is and may disturb the cache. Taken from the Harry Potter series. Often used when warning other cachers to be careful about exposing the location of a cache to non-cachers, when its hiding place is not in a remote location.

**Multi-cache** - A series of caches in which each cache provides coordinates to the next cache (typically a micro) in the series and eventually to a regular cache container. The simplest multi can have one redirector; the hardest can have many, many more.

**Nano** – A nano cache is a cache that is smaller than a micro cache. Commonly magnetic and not much larger than the size of a pencil eraser.

**Numbers Run** – When a group of cachers is out to find as many caches as possible in one day.

**Park 'n Grab** – (PnG) A term used to describe a cache located close to a parking area and requires little walking.

**Power Trail** – A path with a large number of caches. Caches can be placed every 1/10 of a mile. These trails allow cachers to easily increase their find count.

**Puzzle or Mystery Cache** – These caches involve solving complicated puzzles to determine the coordinates of the cache. Puzzles commonly include trivia, ciphers or mathematical puzzles.

**Rain Gauge Cache (RGC)** – This type of cache is hidden in a pipe that requires you to fill the pipe with water and float the cache to the top.

**Redirector** - A cache which only contains a set of coordinates in order to send the seeker to the actual cache being hunted.

**ROT13** – The type of cipher used to hide the hints for a geocache on geocaching.com. Similar to Caesar Ciphers, ROT13 shifts the letters of the alphabet down thirteen characters.

Cipher Key - Letter above equals below, and vice versa.

```
A B C D E F G H I J K L M
N O P Q R S T U V W X Y Z
```

**SBA** – Should be archived. A log indicating that there is a severe problem with the cache, and should be removed.

**Spoiler** - A hint to make finding a cache easier.

**Signature Item** - Something unique that a particular geocacher always places in a cache.

**Swag** - Slang term for the treasure and trinkets found in a geocache. Commonly thought to stand for Stuff We All Get.

**TFTC** - Thanks For The Cache.

**TFTH** – Thanks For The Hide.

**TNLN** - Took Nothing, Left Nothing. The cacher did not exchange an item from the cache contents.

**TNLNSL** - Took Nothing, Left Nothing, Signed Log. Similar to TNLN above, but also indicating that they signed the cache's logbook.

**Travel Bug** - An item passed from cache to cache. Travel bugs are assigned tracking numbers and their travels can be tracked online. Many travel bugs have stated goals, such as making its way to a specific city or country.

**Travel Bug Hotel** – A geocache with the purpose of acting as an exchange point for travel bugs and geocoins.

**URP** - Unnatural Rock Pile. Refers to common practice of stacking rocks on top of the cache to hide its location. The resulting pile often stands out from natural formations.

**Virtual** - Refers to a virtual cache, which does not represent a hidden container, but instead, a location or monument that the cacher is supposed to find. Virtual caches are confirmed by answering a question posed by the cache owner in the description.

**WAAS** – Stands for Wide Area Augmentation System. Uses a series of ground stations to send corrective data to satellites, increasing the accuracy of GPS units.

*www.GeocachingClassroom.com*

**Watch List** – A watch list is a list of users watching a particular cache, or travel bug. If you are on the watch list you will receive an email each time a new log is entered.

**Waypoint** – A physical location on earth. Waypoints are defined by a set of coordinates that include longitude, latitude and altitude.

**WGS84** – Stands for World Geodetic System of 1984 and is the current geodetic datum used for GPS.

**XNSL** - Exchanged Nothing, Signed Log. A variation on TNLNSL

**YAPIDKA** - Yet Another Park I Didn't Know About. Refers to the fact that some caches bring people to parts of town they know little about.

## Degree of Confluence Project

The goal of the project is to visit each of the latitude and longitude integer degree intersections in the world, and to take pictures at each location. Look for pictures and stories about the visits at www.confluence.org.

*Chapter 6*

# Understanding the Garmin GPS

Garmin GPS devices are fairly rugged. However, these precision devices, actually contain small computers that should be handled with care. Never subject your GPS to extreme heat, such as the inside of a closed car during the summer months. When you are not using the GPS for a long period of time, remove the batteries. The Garmin Etrex is water resistant, however it will not float. For this reason, I recommend getting the bright yellow case because it would be easier to find in the water.

In order for your Garmin GPS to work properly it will require an unobstructed view of the sky. The GPS will not work inside, or underground. When used in an area of heavy tree cover, the accuracy will degrade.

The actual battery life of the GPS is between 10-15 hours on a fresh set of alkaline batteries. Always carry a spare set of AA batteries when caching. Using AA batteries is an excellent feature of the Etrex. AA batteries are the most popular size in the world and can be found in most convenience stores.

## SOFTWARE UPDATES

You should update the software on your GPS to be sure it is up to date. Garmin provides free firmware updates for all of its GPS units. To update your GPS you must download the Garmin Webupdate software from:

http://www8.garmin.com/products/webupdater/

For a direct link visit: www.GeocachingClassroom.com.

After downloading the software be sure your GPS has a new set of batteries before starting the update. Then simply attach your GPS to your computer with a USB cable and start the program. Then follow the online prompts.

*Geocaching with a Garmin GPS*

# Garmin GPS Functions

In this section you will learn how to quickly access all of the essential geocaching features of your Garmin Etrex. Have your GPS in hand and try each feature as you read.

##  Turning it On

Turn on the GPS by pressing and holding the power button for two seconds. Release the power button when the startup screen appears. The satellite page will appear. The satellite page shows the relative position of the satellites above. Normally it will take a few minutes for the GPS receiver to lock in on the satellites. A GPS needs a clear view of the sky. If you are indoors the GPS will not be able to receive the satellite signals. When enough satellite signals are received, the map page will appear showing your current location.

There are three main pages on the Garmin Etrex: Compass, Map, and Main Menu. Press the *Quit* key on the right side of the GPS. Each time you press the *Quit* key you will move to the next page.

## COMPASS PAGE

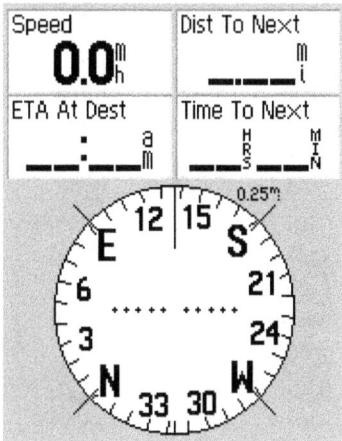

The compass page will show your bearing and up to four other data fields. To customize the compass page press the *Find* Key and select *Change Data Fields*.

## Geodashing

Geodashing is a game in which players use GPS receivers on a playing field that covers the entire planet. The Waypoints, or dashpoints, to be reached are randomly selected. The win goes to the one who can get to the most dashpoints; that is, if you can get to them at all! For more information visit http://geodashing.gpsgames.org/

# Main Menu

The Main Menu provides a directory of other menus and features. It also contains the battery meter in the upper right corner of the screen.

# Map Page

The Map Page displays your current location as a black triangle. The map page shows your longitude and latitude, Waypoints, and movements.

##  Power/Backlight Key

Press and hold the *Power/Backlight Key* for 2 seconds to turn the unit on or off. Quickly press and release to adjust the backlighting, view the date or time, and view the battery capacity. Using the backlight will consume the battery power faster. When the batteries are almost depleted the backlight will not be available.

##  Quit Key

Press the *Quit* Key to cycle through the main pages. Press and release to cancel any entry or exit a page.

## Zoom In/Out Keys

The top two buttons on the left-hand side are used to zoom in or out on the map page. The bottom button zooms in to display more detail. The top button zooms out for less detail and to view a larger area.

Press the *Quit* Key button until the map page appears. Press the *Zoom in* button until the GPS is zoomed in as much as possible. The scale on the lower left should display 20 feet. This scale is comparable to you hovering 20 feet off the ground looking down.

Now *Zoom out* until the scale says 120 miles. You should be able to see the outline of your state. This zoom level is like hovering 120 miles above your current location.

*Geocaching with a Garmin GPS*  51

#  Find Key

This key has many functions depending on how long you hold the key in and what page you are on.

From the Map Page press the *Find* key once and a menu will appear allowing you to change the map page settings.

From the Map Page, if you hold the *Find* key for **two seconds** the Find Page will appear. From this menu you can find Waypoints and Geocaches. You can also access the Find Menu from the Main Menu page.

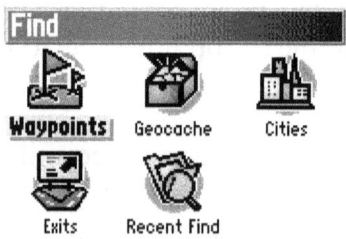

*www.GeocachingClassroom.com*

From the Find Page press and **hold** the *Find* key to see a list of the Waypoints and caches you have recently found.

From the compass page press the *Find* key once, and select *Change Data Fields* to customize the compass display page.

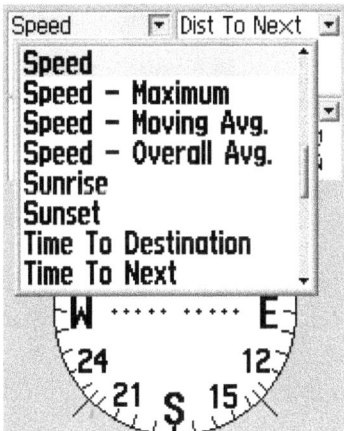

*Geocaching with a Garmin GPS*   53

## Enter/Rocker Key

The Enter/Rocker key is similar to a computer mouse. It allows you to make selections on different menus and pan left/right and up/down on the map page. You can also push **IN** to make selections of highlighted areas. Pushing **IN** on the Rocker/Enter Key is like pressing the right mouse key when using a computer. When on the map page, press **IN** and hold for two seconds to mark your current location as a Waypoint.

## Satellite Page

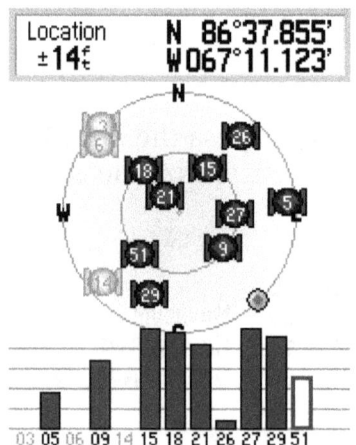

Press the *Quit* key until the Main Menu appears. Satellite should be highlighted. Push **IN** on the Enter/Rocker key to enter the Satellite page. The circles provide a visual reference of the satellite signals being received. The bar at the bottom shows the signal strength, accuracy, and the number of satellites signals. To geocache successfully you need signals from three or more satellites.

If you have a GPS with a color screen, press the *Find* key and select multicolor. The satellite and graph bars will appear in color.

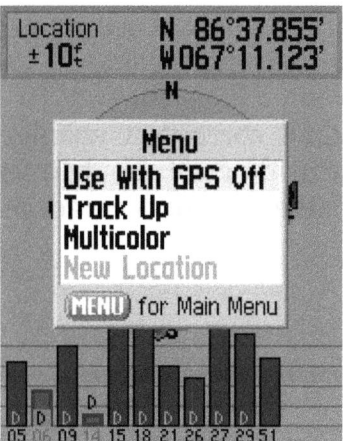

## WAAS

There are 24+ satellites in space. These satellites orbit the Earth every 12 hours in 6 different planes. To determine a 3-D position the GPS unit must receive at least four satellites. The GPS can determine your longitude, latitude and altitude. GPS units have an accuracy of 15 meters using the 24 satellites. Using WAAS this accuracy increases to better than 3 meters.

GPS units do not send signals; they receive them. The GPS is actually a computer that receives and measures the distance between the GPS and several satellites.

The Wide Area Augmentation System (WAAS) is made up of approximately 25 ground stations in North America. These stations send out a signal to satellites that makes corrections for errors caused by ionosphere disturbances, timing and satellite orbit errors.

Enabling WAAS on your GPS usually will improve the accuracy of your GPS. WAAS will only work if you are receiving a signal from WAAS satellites. After you have turned

*Geocaching with a Garmin GPS*  55

on your GPS and the Map Page appears, check how many satellite signals you are receiving by going to the satellite page. Looking at the satellite page, a geo-stationary WAAS correction satellite will have a number higher than 32. If you are receiving this signal you will see small D's appear at the bottom of the satellite strength bars.

Using this differential correction enables the GPS to get maximum accuracy readings of about 10 feet. The top of the satellite page shows the current accuracy and your location.

---

### Hide + Seek

This geocaching thing is not really a new idea. Kids have been playing hide and seek for hundred of years. Pirates have been known to bury their treasures and hide their maps. Over 100 years ago, something similar to geocaching appeared in England, called letterboxing. A letterbox contained a logbook, and a stamp or punch. Clues were distributed leading to the container's location. When found, you would sign the logbook, and stamp your personal logbook with the stamp in the letterbox. Letterboxing continues today throughout the world. To find a letterbox near you visit www.letterboxing.org.

## Marking a Waypoint

When you download a set of geocache coordinates you are actually downloading a Waypoint. A Waypoint is simply a point in space. Geocache Waypoints usually appear as the treasure chest icon.

After you mark or save a Waypoint on the GPS it is easy to navigate back to that location. To mark a Waypoint:

1. Turn on the GPS receiver.
2. Walk to the position you want to save.
3. Press **IN** on the Enter/Rocker Key until the Waypoint page appears.
4. The GPS will automatically assign a three-digit number to the Waypoint.

You can customize the name of the Waypoint and add additional information by using the Enter/Rocker Key. Use the Enter/Rocker Key to highlight the area you wish to change. Then push **IN** and the on screen keyboard will appear. Enter the new information by selecting each letter using the Enter/Rocker Key. Click OK when finished.

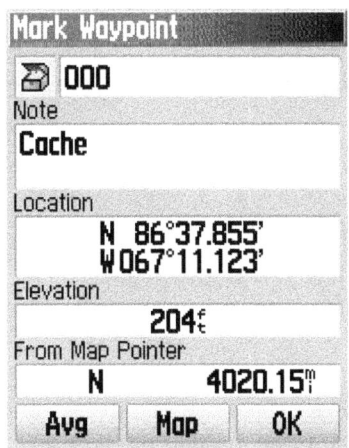

*Geocaching with a Garmin GPS*

## HIDING CACHES

When hiding caches you want the most accurate location possible. To record the most accurate position, highlight and click on the *AVG* Button on the lower left. This will allow the GPS to average the signals from all the satellites. It will also show you the accuracy of the recorded location in the upper left had corner.

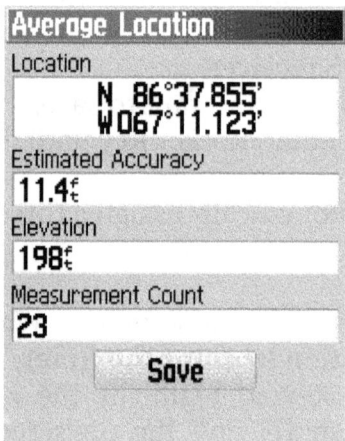

### Trekking

Depending on your journey, a good walking stick can make geocaching much easier, especially when navigating uneven terrain. They are also useful for poking around rocks and fallen logs to scare away any creepy crawly animals.

## FINDING A WAYPOINT OR GEOCACHE

The GPS can direct you to any previously saved Waypoint. To navigate back to a previously saved Waypoint or Geocache follow these steps:

1. From the Map Page, Press the *Find* key on the side of the GPS for two seconds and the Find page will appear. You can also get to the Find page from the Main Menu. But holding the Find key is faster.

2. Highlight Waypoints and push **IN** on the Enter/Rocker key.

3. The Waypoints recorded in the GPS receiver will appear. The closest Waypoint will appear at the top of the screen. Highlight one and push **IN** on the rocker key.

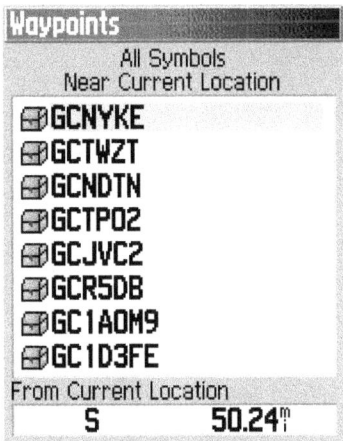

*Geocaching with a Garmin GPS*       59

4. Map and Goto appears at the bottom of the screen. If you click *Goto* you will get compass or driving directions to the Waypoint or cache. If you are looking for a geocache it is more useful to click *Map*.

5. When you click *Map* the map page will appear with the geocache or Waypoint highlighted. This will show your location and the Waypoint or Geocache location. The top right of the screen will show the distance to the Waypoint/Geocache and on the left, the longitude and latitude coordinates of the cache.

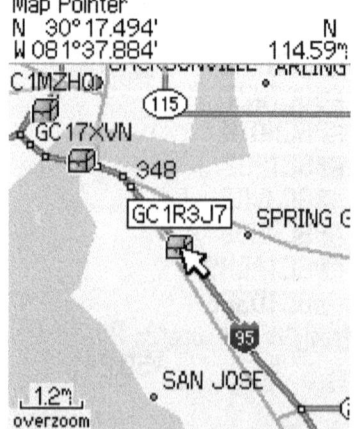

## Manually Entering Geocaches

One way to put a Waypoint or Geocache into your GPS is manually, one number at a time. This is not the easiest method, but you should learn how to do this because there are times when you will need to manually put in the longitude and latitude. For example, if you are looking for a multicache or puzzle cache, you will need to manually update the coordinates for each step.

To manually enter a Waypoint or the location of a geocache press **IN** and hold the *Enter/Rocker* key to access the mark Waypoint screen. Using the Enter/Rocker key, highlight and select *location field* on the mark Waypoint page. Push **IN** on the *Enter/Rocker* key and the on screen keypad will appear. Using the Enter/Rocker key, enter the new coordinates, highlight and press *OK* when finished.

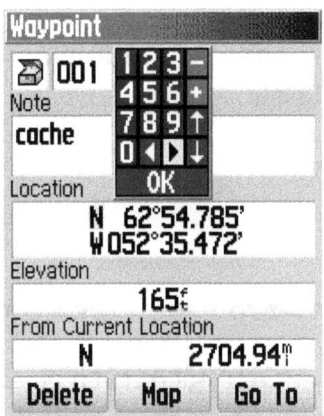

In the United States the first coordinate will always have N for North. The second coordinate will always have a W for West.

By default, Waypoints are given a three-digit number. You may use the Enter/Rocker key to highlight any field to enter custom information. It's a good idea to change the marker from the default blue flag and place additional information in the note field. If you are hiding a cache, use the treasure chest symbol.

*Geocaching with a Garmin GPS*

## DELETING WAYPOINTS

From the main menu click *Find*, then *Waypoints*. Highlight the Waypoint you want to *delete*. Push in on the *Rocker/Enter* key and select delete. To delete all the Waypoint/Geocaches, from the Waypoint page, press the *Find* key, and then select *Delete*.

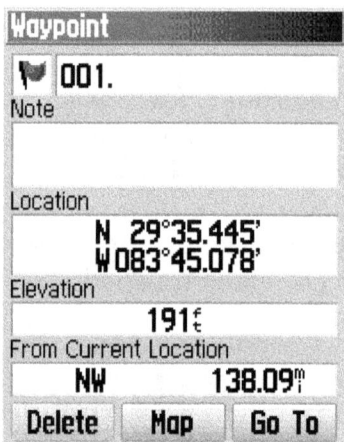

## Your Statistics

Geocaching statistics refers to the number of caches you have found and hidden. Other members can check your statistics. The number of caches you have found appears next to your geocaching alias. Some geocachers are competitive and attempt to increase their find number by going on numbers runs. A numbers run is when geocachers attempt to find as many caches as possible in one day.

#  TRACKS

Tracks are a very important feature for geocachers and hikers. Before heading out on a hike, or leaving your car behind to look for a cache be sure to turn on this feature. Select *Tracks* from the main menu. Turn on the track log using the Enter/Rocker key. Also clear the old track log.

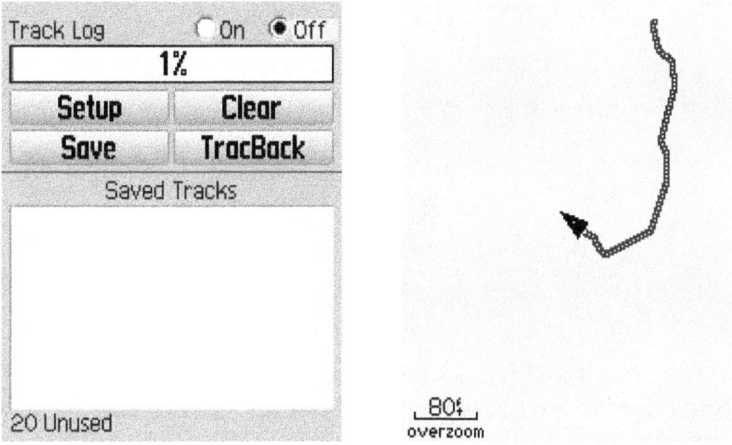

The track log starts recording as soon as the unit gets a location fix. The percentage of memory used by the track log appears at the top of the tracks page.

This feature will place a dashed line on the map page showing your path. It's like leaving digital breadcrumbs! For geocachers, this helps us find our car after a long hike to find a cache. It also lets us know if we have been walking in circles around a cache. You may change the color of the track, on the setup page.

*Save* allows you to save your track or journey to the GPS. On some units you can record the track log on the removable Micro SD memory card. Using this method allows you to record a large number of track points.

Also, if wrap when full is checked, it will wrap new points over the top of old points when the maximum memory is reached. If unchecked it will turn off the track log when memory is full.

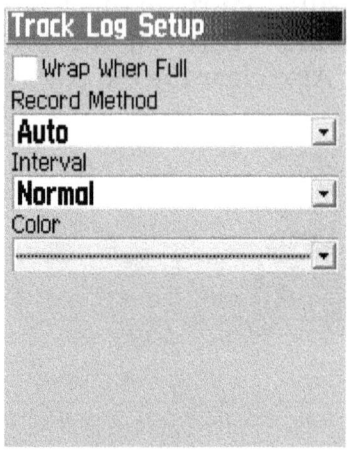

If you have recorded tracks along your journey you can use the TracBack feature to return to any point along the journey. From the track log select *TracBack*, and then select a point to return to. The GPS will give you step by step directions to return to that point.

For geocaching you probably don't need the tracback feature. Simply having the track on screen will be enough to know if you are going in circles around the cache, and you'll be able to retrace your steps back to the car.

## RECENT FINDS

To view recent geocaches or Waypoints you have found, from the Map Page hold the *Find* button in for two seconds. When the Find Menu appears, hold the *Find* button in again for two seconds and the Recent Finds screen will appear.

### The First Geocache

Dave Ulmer placed the first geocache on May 3, 2000. It contained a Delorme Topo USA map on 2 CD Roms, a cassette recorder, a *George of the Jungle* VHS tape, a Ross Perot book, four $1 bills, a slingshot handle, and a can of beans.

*Geocaching with a Garmin GPS*

## Chapter 7
# Setting up for Geocaching

### SETUP

From the Main Menu select *Setup*. The setup menu will appear. There are a few settings important to geocachers, although many are personal preference. Check the following items from the Setup Menu.

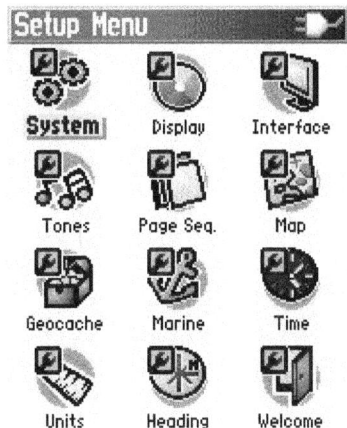

---

### The Garmin Chirp

The chirp is a wireless beacon designed specifically for the outdoor adventures of geocaching. Durable and waterproof, the chirp communicates with compatible Garmin GPS units. The cache hider can program the chirp to give out hints and coordinates when the geocacher gets within 30 feet of the chirp. The chirp also keeps track of the number of visitors to the cache.

*Geocaching with a Garmin GPS*

#  SYSTEM

Under this menu be sure WAAS/EGNOS is enabled. This will provide a more accurate position fix. Also, select the battery type you are using.

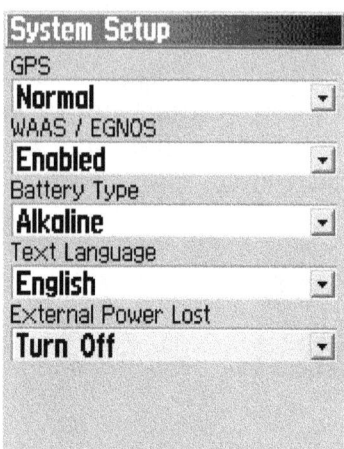

# DISPLAY

In this menu, I change the *Backlight Timeout* to *Stays On*. When looking for a cache, it's frustrating to look down at your GPS when the screen has gone dim.

Doing this uses up more battery power, so always keep a spare set of AA batteries on hand.

 *www.GeocachingClassroom.com*

## Page Sequence

You can set which menu pages appears each time you press the page button. The default is Compass, Map, and Main Menu.

I added the satellite page to the rotation. This lets you quickly see the strength and number of satellites being received. Adding too many pages can really slow you down, so **don't** click *Include All*.

#  MAP

Select *North Up* for orientation. This keeps North at the top of the GPS. Selecting *Track Up* keeps your direction of travel at the top of the GPS. Selecting *Track Up* when zoomed into a geocache is very frustrating. The map bounces around trying to keep your direction of travel at the top of the screen. If you feel your GPS is acting strange when geocaching, check to see that this setting is set for *Track Up* orientation.

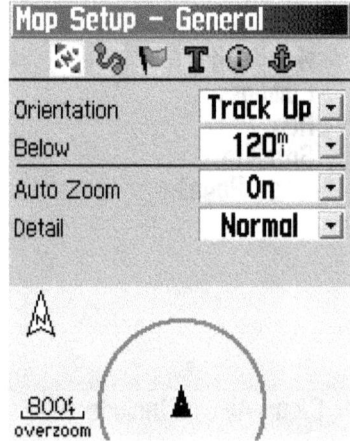

##  Geocache

Select *YES* so that the icon changes to an open treasure chest and makes a calendar entry, when you find the cache.

## Units

If you're geocaching, it is critical that the map datum is correct. Be sure that the map datum is set to WGS 84, otherwise you will not be able to find the cache.

Also, use the Position Format hdddd mm.mmm, which is the standard for GPS receivers (like the Garmin eTrex).

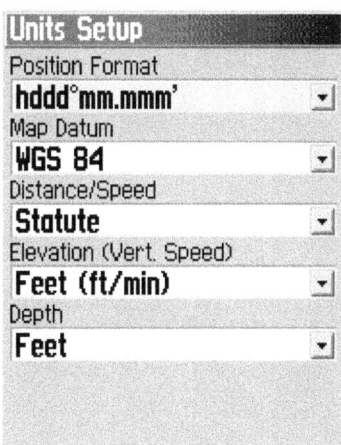

## Welcome Message

You can type in a welcome message that appears when the GPS starts. This is good if you have more than one GPS. Typing in a different welcome message will allow you to tell them apart.

 www.GeocachingClassroom.com

## Trip Computer

From the main menu select *Trip Comp*. The trip computer shows eight types of navigation data. Each field is selectable and can contain one of many optional fields. To change the data in the field press the *Find* key and *select Change Data Fields*.

Also, from the same menu, be sure to reset the trip computer before starting a new adventure.

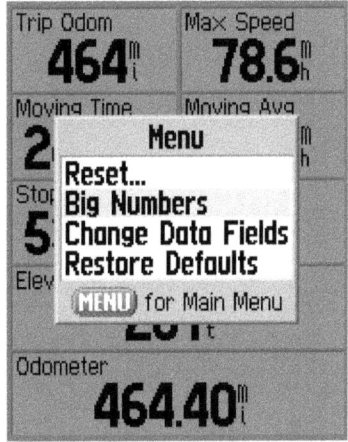

Code 96931

*Geocaching with a Garmin GPS*

## Chapter 8

# Geocaching with the Garmin GPS

## MANAGING GEOCACHING FILES

Transferring Waypoints to your computer and additional GPS's is simple using EasyGPS.

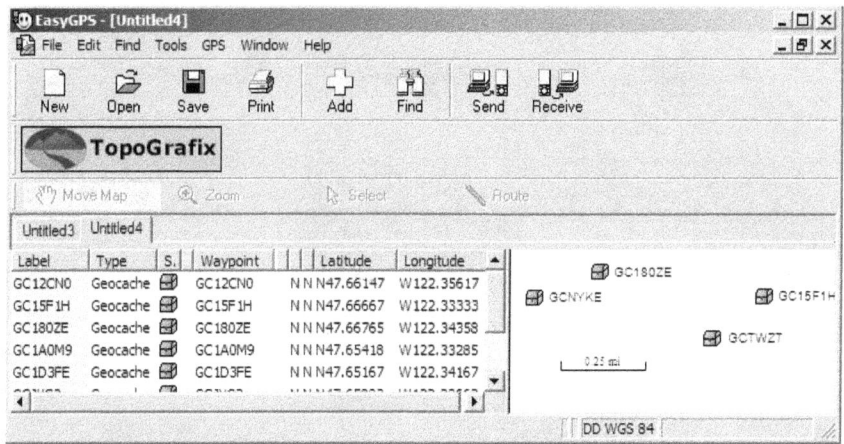

I usually do this after each long journey. For example, after returning from the Grand Canyon I saved all of the caches to a file called, "Grand Canyon Vacation." This gives me more room on my GPS and saved the caches for future use. I can also share the files with someone who may visit the Grand Canyon area.

Follow these instructions to transfer files to your computer.

1. Start the EasyGPS program and plug in your GPS with the USB cable. The *Select a GPS Receiver* dialog box will appear. Click *Add GPS* and select your GPS unit, then click *OK*.

*Geocaching with a Garmin GPS*

# Download EasyGPS from EasyGPS.com

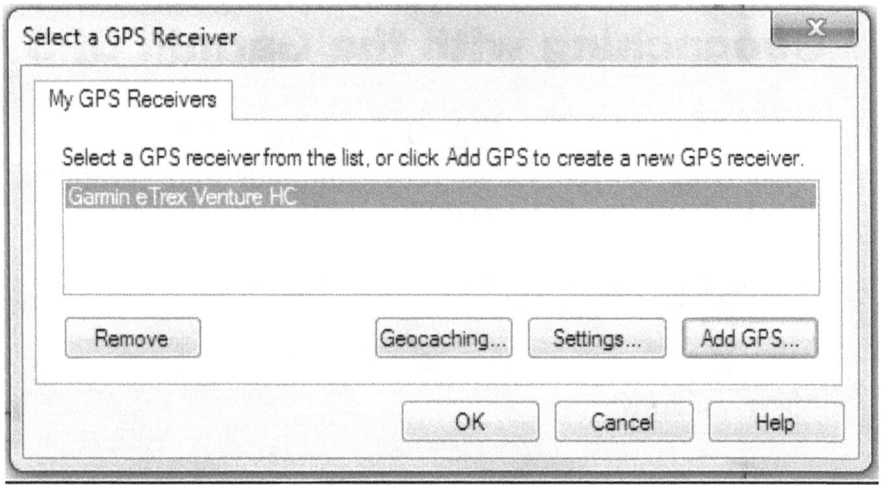

From the top of the EasyGPS screen click *Receive*. From the *Receive from GPS* dialog box select *Waypoint* and *Geocaches*, then *OK*.

All of the Waypoint files on your GPS will be copied into the EasyGPS screen. Now, click *File* and *Save*. Give this set of Waypoints a unique name, for example, "Grand Canyon Vacation."

*www.GeocachingClassroom.com*

## Transferring GPS Files

Now, to transfer the Waypoints to another GPS, simply disconnect the original GPS and hook up another with the USB cable and click *Send*. All of the Waypoints will be transferred to the new GPS. To see if they are actually there, hold the *Find* button in for two seconds until the *Find Menu* appears. Then push **IN** on the *Rocker/Enter Key*.

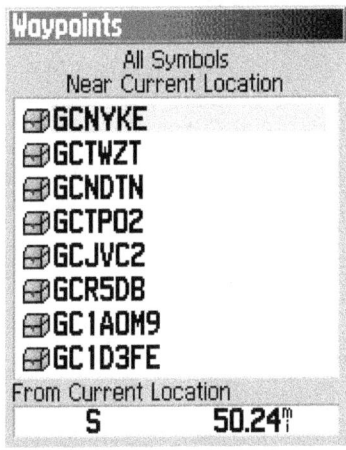

You should then see a list of Waypoints on the new GPS.

Hint: From EasyGPS you can edit the names and notes given for each cache. The names and notes will appear on the GPS. Use the note area to provide clues or general locations of the cache. It is easier to enter notes using your computer keyboard than the onscreen keypad of the GPS. After adding notes simply send the files back to the GPS unit.

*Geocaching with a Garmin GPS*

## Loading Caches from GeoCaching.com

Sending files from www.Geocaching.com to your GPS is easy. From the Cache page simply click on *Send to GPS*. A dialog box will appear and the GPS unit attached to your computer should be recognized. If the GPS is not found, click on *Garmin Communicator* and install the software. After installing the software your GPS will appear in the dialog box. To send the cache location click *Write*. You must click *Write* for each cache you wish to send to the GPS.

```
Found eTrex Venture HC (Unit ID 3382470288)
   Find Devices
  Write    Cancel Write
Powered by Garmin Communicator
```

## Transferring Saved Files

If your GPS is not supported by the "Send to GPS" feature on Geocaching.com you can save .LOC files to your computer and then use EasyGPS to move them to your GPS. When saving files to your computer be sure to remember what folder or directory they are saved in.

Open the easy GPS program. Then open one of the .LOC files. After connecting your GPS to the computer click *Send* from the top menu bar. Open each file and click *Send* until all the .LOC files are loaded into the GPS. After all the files are loaded into the GPS click *Receive*. All of the .LOC files from the GPS will now appear on one EasyGPS screen. You can then click file *Save As* and save all the caches to a single master file.

# Viewing Caches with Google Earth

Google Earth is a virtual globe made up of satellite images of the Earth called tiles. The program allows you to fly around a virtual Earth complete with zoom, rotate and tilt features. The level of detail varies depending on the location.

First download and install Google Earth from:

**http://www.google.com/earth/index.html**

1. Launch Google Earth by double clicking on its icon.

2. Moving around: The most common way to move is to click the mouse and drag the Earth around. You can also use the navigation controls in the upper right corner of the screen.

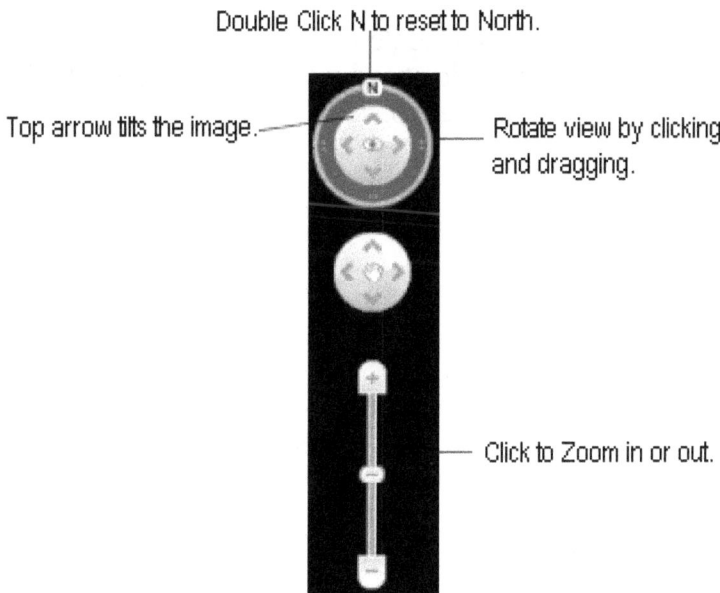

3. Zooming – The long slider on the controls allows you to zoom in and out of a location.

*Geocaching with a Garmin GPS*

4. Finding a location – If you know the approximate location of a town, river or other landmark its easy to find by zooming in and moving around the Earth.

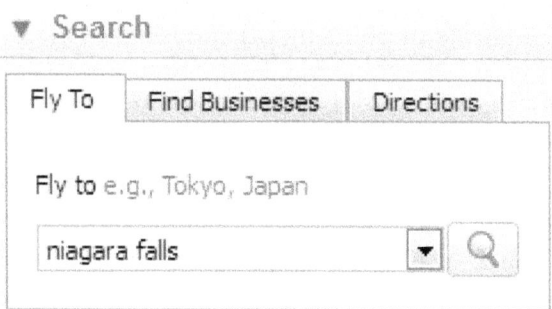

5. To find a well-known location use the search box. For example, if you're looking for Niagara Falls, simply type it in the search box and click the magnifying glass and Google Earth will take you there. You can also put the coordinates in the search box.

6. At the bottom of the Google Earth window you will see the longitude and latitude coordinates. For Niagara Falls the coordinates are   43° 4'40.57"N   79° 4'33.33"W

**Viewing Caches**
If you enjoy geocaching, being able to see the caches in Google Earth can really help!

Google Earth supports files called KML files. KML stands for Keyhole Markup Language. A KML file is specifically formatted for Google Earth. The KML data file from Geocaching.com contains information such as geocache name, type, terrain and difficulty rating.

Using Google Earth and the geocaching KML file makes selecting and loading caches to your GPS easy.

*www.GeocachingClassroom.com*

To use the viewer:

1. First download and install Google Earth. Then, download the KML file from Geocaching.com. To do this log into your Geocaching.com account. You'll need to sign up for an account if you don't already have one. The basic level account is FREE and all you will need until you really get into geocaching.

2. From the "My Profile" section download the viewer. It is located at the bottom right hand corner of the screen. Click on *Download Viewer* then click *open*.

   **Geocache Google Earth Viewer**

   • Download Viewer*

   *How to View Geocaches Using Google Earth

3. After the viewer downloads it will automatically open Google Earth.

4. Now, using Google Earth, zoom into your neighborhood (type your address in the search box and click the magnifying glass). You should see several green geocache icons appear. Click on one.

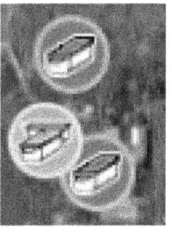

As you click on the icon, the cache summary will appear. You will see the size, difficulty and terrain ratings. If you want more information, click on the *Geocache GC number*. A browser window will appear in the lower section of Google Earth, and the full cache information page will appear.

5. In the browser window you can read the details about the cache and download the coordinates directly to your GPS. Connect your GPS to the computer and click *Send to GPS*. Note: you must be logged into your geocaching account in order to see and send the coordinates to your GPS.

The geocaching Google Earth viewer allows you to see up to 500 geocaches within one map view. If the view has more than 500 caches, you will see a random sampling of 500 caches.

Currently basic members can view 25 pages per day. Premium members can view 250 pages per day. To see how many page views you have used, expand the geocaching viewer by clicking the + button.

You can change your default settings so that panning does not automatically update the map. Anytime the map updates, it is counted as a page view. Your 25 page views a day can go fast if you don't do this.

On the left-hand side of the screen in *Places,* right click on *Geocaching Google Earth Viewer,* then select *Properties.* Click on the *refresh* tab. Under *View Based Refresh,* change it to **On Request,** then select *OK.*

# Geocaching Links

Below are links to popular geocaching websites. For an up to date list and direct links visit GeocachingClassroom.com

## Top Geocaching Websites

GeoCaching.com
WayMarking.com
TerraCaching.com
NaviCache.com

## Software and Geocaching Utilities

EasyGPS.com
ExpertGPS.com
GSAK.net
Google.com/Earth

## GPS and Map Manufacturers

Bushnell.com
DeLorme.com
Garmin.com
Lowrance.com
Magellan.com
Trimble.com

## Money Trackers

Canada - CDN-Money.ca
Canada - WheresWilly.com
USA - WheresGeorge.com
Europe - en.euroBillTracker.com

**Geochecker.com** – Use this site to check the coordinates of a geocache.

**GeocachingPolicy.info** – Wondering if you can place a geocache in a park or national forest? This website lists the known policies of local and national land and facility managers.

**EarthCache.org** – Provides a listing of Earth caches around the world.

**Handicaching.com** – Is a site dedicated to improve the accessibility of geocaching for disabled people all over the world.

**GPSgames.org** – This site creates GPS related games.

**LetterBoxing.org** - Letterboxing originated long before GPS existed. Similar to geocaching, Letterboxing uses only written directions.

**Trails.com** – The source for trail guides and topographic maps.

**Confluence.org** - The Degree Confluence Project - The goal of this project is to visit each of the latitude and longitude integer degree intersections in the world, and to take pictures at each location. The pictures, and stories about the visits, are posted at confluence.org.

**Orienteering.org** - Orienteering is a sport that requires navigational skills using a map and compass to navigate from point to point.

# Index

## A

ALR · 39
Archived · 39
ATCF · 39
Attribute · 39

## B

Backlight · 5, 51, 68
Battery · 35
Benchmark · 5, 27, 39
Bison Tube · 39
Breeder Cache · 39
Bushnell.com · 85
BYOP · 39

## C

Cache Find Log · 88
Cache Machine · 40
Cache Rating · 40
Caches Hidden Log · 89
Canada · 30, 85
CITO · 40
Coastal Survey · 27
Compass · 5, 48, 49, 69
Compass Page · 5, 49
Confluence.org · 86

## D

D/T · 40
Data Fields · 49, 53, 73
Datum · 40, 45
Dave Ulmer · 65
Degree of Confluence Project · 45
DeLorme.com · 85
Dipping · 37, 40
Display setup · 6, 68
DNF · 40

## E

EarthCache · 14, 40, 86
EarthCache.org · 14, 86
EasyGPS · 75, 76, 77, 78, 85
Encrypting · 24
Etrex · 47, 48
Event Cache · 14, 40
ExpertGPS.com · 85

## F

FAA · 30, 36
Find Key · 6, 49, 52
Find Score · 41
Finding a Waypoint · 6, 59
Fire Tacks · 41
First to Find · 33, 41
Florida · 2, 3, 22, 25
FTF Token · 41

## G

Garmin · 1, 2, 4, 5, 6, 47, 48, 67, 71, 75, 78, 85
Garmin Communicator · 78
Garmin.com · 85
GC Code · 41, 81, 88, 89
Geocache · 5, 6, 7, 8, 10, 15, 16, 21, 31, 32, 33, 34, 37, 40, 41, 43, 44, 54, 57, 59, 60, 61, 65, 70, 71, 78, 80, 81, 86, 88, 89
Geocache Series · 41
Geocaching Files · 6
Geocaching.com · 2, 4, 6, 15, 16, 17, 26, 27, 34, 78, 80, 81
GeocachingPolicy.info · 86
Geochecker.com · 86
Geocoin · 37, 41
Geodashing · 49
Georace.net · 23, 33
Geotoken · 5, 7, 23, 33, 41

Geotrail · 41
Gift cards · 33
Google caching · 41
Google Earth · 2, 3, 6, 11, 41, 79, 80, 81, 82, 83
Goto · 60
GPS · 1, 2, 3, 5, 6, 7, 8, 9, 11, 12, 13, 17, 18, 19, 21, 22, 27, 29, 30, 32, 35, 36, 37, 40, 41, 44, 45, 47, 48, 49, 51, 55, 56, 57, 58, 59, 61, 63, 64, 67, 68, 70, 71, 72, 75, 76, 77, 78, 80, 82, 85, 86, 89
GPSgames.org · 86
GPSr · 41
Ground Zero · 20, 41
GSAK.net · 85
Guard Rail Cache · 41

# *H*

Handicaching.com · 86
Harry Potter · 9, 24, 42
Hide and Seek · 15
Hiding Caches · 6, 58
Hitchhiker · 42
Hydro Cache · 42

# *I*

In plain view · 42
IPV · 42

# *J*

J.K. Rowling · 24

# *K*

KML · 80, 81

# *L*

Lamp Post Cache · 42
Latitude · 15, 88, 89

Letterboxing · 42, 56, 86
Longitude · 15, 88, 89
Lowrance.com · 85

# *M*

Magellan.com · 85
Main Menu · 5, 48, 50, 52, 54, 59, 67, 69
Manually Entering Geocaches · 6, 61
Map page · 5, 6, 17, 48, 50, 52, 56, 59, 60, 65, 69, 70, 85
Map Page · 5, 50, 52, 56, 59, 65
Map setup · 5, 6, 17, 48, 50, 52, 56, 59, 60, 65, 69, 70, 85
Marking a Waypoint · 6, 32, 57
Memory · 36
Mexico · 30
Micro · 14, 42, 63
Micro cache · 14
Micro caches · 14, 42, 63
MKH · 42
Muggler · 5, 9, 24, 42
Multi-Cache · 42

# *N*

Naked Geocaching · 5, 17
Nano · 43
National Parks Service · 31
NaviCache.com · 85
North America · 55
Numbers Run · 43

# *O*

Orienteering.org · 86

# *P*

Paperless · 35, 37
Power Trail · 43
Puzzle · 14, 43
Puzzle Cache · 14

 *www.GeocachingClassroom.com*

## Q

Quit Key · 5, 51

## R

Rain Gauge Cache · 43
Redirector · 43
ROT13 · 43

## S

Satellite · 6, 17, 54
SBA · 43
Schreiver Air Force Base · 30
Screen size · 35
SD memory · 63
Setup menu · 67
Signature item · 23
Simpson Creek · 19
Size · 35
Software · 5, 36, 47, 85
Spoiler · 43
Swag · 44
System setup · 5, 6, 29, 30, 36, 41, 44, 45, 55, 68

## T

TerraCaching.com · 85
TFTC · 44
TFTH · 44
TNLN · 44
TNLNSL · 44, 45
Tracks · 6, 20, 63
Traditional cache · 14
Trails.com · 86
Transferring GPS Files · 6, 77
Transferring Saved Files · 6, 78
Transferring Waypoints · 75
Travel Bug Hotel · 26, 44
Travel bugs · 5, 25, 26, 88
Treasure · 1, 2
Trimble.com · 85
Trip Computer · 6, 73

## U

Units Setup · 6, 71
URP · 44
US Post Office · 31
USB · 36, 47, 75, 77

## V

Virtual · 14, 44
Virtual Cache · 14

## W

WAAS · 6, 30, 36, 44, 55, 68
Watch List · 45
WayMarking.com · 85
Waypoint · 45, 54, 57, 59, 60, 61, 62, 76
Webcam Cache · 14
Weight · 35
Welcome Message · 6, 72
WGS84 · 40, 45
WheresGeorge.com · 85
WheresWilly.com · 85

## X

XNSL · 45

## Y

YAPIDKA · 45

## Z

Zoom in · 6, 17, 51
Zoom out · 51

# Hidden Cache Log

| | |
|---|---|
| Hide Number | |
| Date Hidden | |
| Cache GC Code | |
| Longitude | |
| Latitude | |
| # of Satellites | |
| GPS Accuracy | |
| Notes | |

Cipher Key - Letter above equals below, and vice versa.

```
A B C D E F G H I J K L M
N O P Q R S T U V W X Y Z
```

| | |
|---|---|
| Hide Number | |
| Date Hidden | |
| Cache GC Code | |
| Longitude | |
| Latitude | |
| # of Satellites | |
| GPS Accuracy | |
| Notes | |

www.GeocachingClassroom.com

# Hidden Cache Log

| | |
|---|---|
| Hide Number | |
| Date Hidden | |
| Cache GC Code | |
| Longitude | |
| Latitude | |
| # of Satellites | |
| GPS Accuracy | |
| Notes | |

Cipher Key - Letter above equals below, and vice versa.

```
A B C D E F G H I J K L M
N O P Q R S T U V W X Y Z
```

| | |
|---|---|
| Hide Number | |
| Date Hidden | |
| Cache GC Code | |
| Longitude | |
| Latitude | |
| # of Satellites | |
| GPS Accuracy | |
| Notes | |

*Geocaching with a Garmin GPS*

# Hidden Cache Log

| | |
|---|---|
| Hide Number | |
| Date Hidden | |
| Cache GC Code | |
| Longitude | |
| Latitude | |
| # of Satellites | |
| GPS Accuracy | |
| Notes | |

Cipher Key - Letter above equals below, and vice versa.

```
A B C D E F G H I J K L M
N O P Q R S T U V W X Y Z
```

| | |
|---|---|
| Hide Number | |
| Date Hidden | |
| Cache GC Code | |
| Longitude | |
| Latitude | |
| # of Satellites | |
| GPS Accuracy | |
| Notes | |

*www.GeocachingClassroom.com*

# Hidden Cache Log

| | |
|---|---|
| Hide Number | |
| Date Hidden | |
| Cache GC Code | |
| Longitude | |
| Latitude | |
| # of Satellites | |
| GPS Accuracy | |
| Notes | |

Cipher Key - Letter above equals below, and vice versa.

```
A B C D E F G H I J K L M
N O P Q R S T U V W X Y Z
```

| | |
|---|---|
| Hide Number | |
| Date Hidden | |
| Cache GC Code | |
| Longitude | |
| Latitude | |
| # of Satellites | |
| GPS Accuracy | |
| Notes | |

*Geocaching with a Garmin GPS*

## Hidden Cache Log

| | |
|---|---|
| Hide Number | |
| Date Hidden | |
| Cache GC Code | |
| Longitude | |
| Latitude | |
| # of Satellites | |
| GPS Accuracy | |
| Notes | |

Cipher Key - Letter above equals below, and vice versa.

```
A B C D E F G H I J K L M
N O P Q R S T U V W X Y Z
```

| | |
|---|---|
| Hide Number | |
| Date Hidden | |
| Cache GC Code | |
| Longitude | |
| Latitude | |
| # of Satellites | |
| GPS Accuracy | |
| Notes | |

# Hidden Cache Log

| | |
|---|---|
| Hide Number | |
| Date Hidden | |
| Cache GC Code | |
| Longitude | |
| Latitude | |
| # of Satellites | |
| GPS Accuracy | |
| Notes | |

Cipher Key - Letter above equals below, and vice versa.

```
A  B  C  D  E  F  G  H  I  J  K  L  M
N  O  P  Q  R  S  T  U  V  W  X  Y  Z
```

| | |
|---|---|
| Hide Number | |
| Date Hidden | |
| Cache GC Code | |
| Longitude | |
| Latitude | |
| # of Satellites | |
| GPS Accuracy | |
| Notes | |

*Geocaching with a Garmin GPS*

## Cache Find Log

| | |
|---|---|
| Date | |
| Find Number | |
| Cache Name | |
| Cache GC Code | |
| Latitude | |
| Longitude | |
| Took / Left | |
| Travel Bugs | |
| Notes | |

| | |
|---|---|
| Date | |
| Find Number | |
| Cache Name | |
| Cache GC Code | |
| Latitude | |
| Longitude | |
| Took / Left | |
| Travel Bugs | |
| Notes | |

*www.GeocachingClassroom.com*

## Cache Find Log

| | |
|---|---|
| Date | |
| Find Number | |
| Cache Name | |
| Cache GC Code | |
| Latitude | |
| Longitude | |
| Took / Left | |
| Travel Bugs | |
| Notes | |

| | |
|---|---|
| Date | |
| Find Number | |
| Cache Name | |
| Cache GC Code | |
| Latitude | |
| Longitude | |
| Took / Left | |
| Travel Bugs | |
| Notes | |

*Geocaching with a Garmin GPS*

## Cache Find Log

| | |
|---|---|
| Date | |
| Find Number | |
| Cache Name | |
| Cache GC Code | |
| Latitude | |
| Longitude | |
| Took / Left | |
| Travel Bugs | |
| Notes | |

| | |
|---|---|
| Date | |
| Find Number | |
| Cache Name | |
| Cache GC Code | |
| Latitude | |
| Longitude | |
| Took / Left | |
| Travel Bugs | |
| Notes | |

## Cache Find Log

| | |
|---|---|
| Date | |
| Find Number | |
| Cache Name | |
| Cache GC Code | |
| Latitude | |
| Longitude | |
| Took / Left | |
| Travel Bugs | |
| Notes | |

| | |
|---|---|
| Date | |
| Find Number | |
| Cache Name | |
| Cache GC Code | |
| Latitude | |
| Longitude | |
| Took / Left | |
| Travel Bugs | |
| Notes | |

# Cache Find Log

| | |
|---|---|
| Date | |
| Find Number | |
| Cache Name | |
| Cache GC Code | |
| Latitude | |
| Longitude | |
| Took / Left | |
| Travel Bugs | |
| Notes | |

| | |
|---|---|
| Date | |
| Find Number | |
| Cache Name | |
| Cache GC Code | |
| Latitude | |
| Longitude | |
| Took / Left | |
| Travel Bugs | |
| Notes | |

## Cache Find Log

| | |
|---|---|
| Date | |
| Find Number | |
| Cache Name | |
| Cache GC Code | |
| Latitude | |
| Longitude | |
| Took / Left | |
| Travel Bugs | |
| Notes | |

| | |
|---|---|
| Date | |
| Find Number | |
| Cache Name | |
| Cache GC Code | |
| Latitude | |
| Longitude | |
| Took / Left | |
| Travel Bugs | |
| Notes | |

## Cache Find Log

| | |
|---|---|
| Date | |
| Find Number | |
| Cache Name | |
| Cache GC Code | |
| Latitude | |
| Longitude | |
| Took / Left | |
| Travel Bugs | |
| Notes | |

| | |
|---|---|
| Date | |
| Find Number | |
| Cache Name | |
| Cache GC Code | |
| Latitude | |
| Longitude | |
| Took / Left | |
| Travel Bugs | |
| Notes | |

www.GeocachingClassroom.com

## Cache Find Log

| | |
|---|---|
| Date | |
| Find Number | |
| Cache Name | |
| Cache GC Code | |
| Latitude | |
| Longitude | |
| Took / Left | |
| Travel Bugs | |
| Notes | |

| | |
|---|---|
| Date | |
| Find Number | |
| Cache Name | |
| Cache GC Code | |
| Latitude | |
| Longitude | |
| Took / Left | |
| Travel Bugs | |
| Notes | |

*Geocaching with a Garmin GPS*

## Cache Find Log

| | |
|---|---|
| Date | |
| Find Number | |
| Cache Name | |
| Cache GC Code | |
| Latitude | |
| Longitude | |
| Took / Left | |
| Travel Bugs | |
| Notes | |

| | |
|---|---|
| Date | |
| Find Number | |
| Cache Name | |
| Cache GC Code | |
| Latitude | |
| Longitude | |
| Took / Left | |
| Travel Bugs | |
| Notes | |

## Cache Find Log

| | |
|---|---|
| Date | |
| Find Number | |
| Cache Name | |
| Cache GC Code | |
| Latitude | |
| Longitude | |
| Took / Left | |
| Travel Bugs | |
| Notes | |

| | |
|---|---|
| Date | |
| Find Number | |
| Cache Name | |
| Cache GC Code | |
| Latitude | |
| Longitude | |
| Took / Left | |
| Travel Bugs | |
| Notes | |

## Cache Find Log

| | |
|---|---|
| Date | |
| Find Number | |
| Cache Name | |
| Cache GC Code | |
| Latitude | |
| Longitude | |
| Took / Left | |
| Travel Bugs | |
| Notes | |

| | |
|---|---|
| Date | |
| Find Number | |
| Cache Name | |
| Cache GC Code | |
| Latitude | |
| Longitude | |
| Took / Left | |
| Travel Bugs | |
| Notes | |

## Cache Find Log

| | |
|---|---|
| Date | |
| Find Number | |
| Cache Name | |
| Cache GC Code | |
| Latitude | |
| Longitude | |
| Took / Left | |
| Travel Bugs | |
| Notes | |

| | |
|---|---|
| Date | |
| Find Number | |
| Cache Name | |
| Cache GC Code | |
| Latitude | |
| Longitude | |
| Took / Left | |
| Travel Bugs | |
| Notes | |

*Geocaching with a Garmin GPS*

## Cache Find Log

| | |
|---|---|
| Date | |
| Find Number | |
| Cache Name | |
| Cache GC Code | |
| Latitude | |
| Longitude | |
| Took / Left | |
| Travel Bugs | |
| Notes | |

| | |
|---|---|
| Date | |
| Find Number | |
| Cache Name | |
| Cache GC Code | |
| Latitude | |
| Longitude | |
| Took / Left | |
| Travel Bugs | |
| Notes | |

www.GeocachingClassroom.com

## Cache Find Log

| Date | |
|---|---|
| Find Number | |
| Cache Name | |
| Cache GC Code | |
| Latitude | |
| Longitude | |
| Took / Left | |
| Travel Bugs | |
| Notes | |

| Date | |
|---|---|
| Find Number | |
| Cache Name | |
| Cache GC Code | |
| Latitude | |
| Longitude | |
| Took / Left | |
| Travel Bugs | |
| Notes | |

*Geocaching with a Garmin GPS*

## Cache Find Log

| | |
|---|---|
| Date | |
| Find Number | |
| Cache Name | |
| Cache GC Code | |
| Latitude | |
| Longitude | |
| Took / Left | |
| Travel Bugs | |
| Notes | |

| | |
|---|---|
| Date | |
| Find Number | |
| Cache Name | |
| Cache GC Code | |
| Latitude | |
| Longitude | |
| Took / Left | |
| Travel Bugs | |
| Notes | |

*www.GeocachingClassroom.com*

# Cache Find Log

| | |
|---|---|
| Date | |
| Find Number | |
| Cache Name | |
| Cache GC Code | |
| Latitude | |
| Longitude | |
| Took / Left | |
| Travel Bugs | |
| Notes | |

| | |
|---|---|
| Date | |
| Find Number | |
| Cache Name | |
| Cache GC Code | |
| Latitude | |
| Longitude | |
| Took / Left | |
| Travel Bugs | |
| Notes | |

*Geocaching with a Garmin GPS*

## Cache Find Log

| | |
|---|---|
| Date | |
| Find Number | |
| Cache Name | |
| Cache GC Code | |
| Latitude | |
| Longitude | |
| Took / Left | |
| Travel Bugs | |
| Notes | |

| | |
|---|---|
| Date | |
| Find Number | |
| Cache Name | |
| Cache GC Code | |
| Latitude | |
| Longitude | |
| Took / Left | |
| Travel Bugs | |
| Notes | |

## Cache Find Log

| | |
|---|---|
| Date | |
| Find Number | |
| Cache Name | |
| Cache GC Code | |
| Latitude | |
| Longitude | |
| Took / Left | |
| Travel Bugs | |
| Notes | |

| | |
|---|---|
| Date | |
| Find Number | |
| Cache Name | |
| Cache GC Code | |
| Latitude | |
| Longitude | |
| Took / Left | |
| Travel Bugs | |
| Notes | |

## Cache Find Log

| | |
|---|---|
| Date | |
| Find Number | |
| Cache Name | |
| Cache GC Code | |
| Latitude | |
| Longitude | |
| Took / Left | |
| Travel Bugs | |
| Notes | |

| | |
|---|---|
| Date | |
| Find Number | |
| Cache Name | |
| Cache GC Code | |
| Latitude | |
| Longitude | |
| Took / Left | |
| Travel Bugs | |
| Notes | |

## Cache Find Log

| | |
|---|---|
| Date | |
| Find Number | |
| Cache Name | |
| Cache GC Code | |
| Latitude | |
| Longitude | |
| Took / Left | |
| Travel Bugs | |
| Notes | |

| | |
|---|---|
| Date | |
| Find Number | |
| Cache Name | |
| Cache GC Code | |
| Latitude | |
| Longitude | |
| Took / Left | |
| Travel Bugs | |
| Notes | |

*Geocaching with a Garmin GPS*

## Cache Find Log

| | |
|---|---|
| Date | |
| Find Number | |
| Cache Name | |
| Cache GC Code | |
| Latitude | |
| Longitude | |
| Took / Left | |
| Travel Bugs | |
| Notes | |

| | |
|---|---|
| Date | |
| Find Number | |
| Cache Name | |
| Cache GC Code | |
| Latitude | |
| Longitude | |
| Took / Left | |
| Travel Bugs | |
| Notes | |

www.GeocachingClassroom.com

## Cache Find Log

| | |
|---|---|
| Date | |
| Find Number | |
| Cache Name | |
| Cache GC Code | |
| Latitude | |
| Longitude | |
| Took / Left | |
| Travel Bugs | |
| Notes | |

| | |
|---|---|
| Date | |
| Find Number | |
| Cache Name | |
| Cache GC Code | |
| Latitude | |
| Longitude | |
| Took / Left | |
| Travel Bugs | |
| Notes | |

*Geocaching with a Garmin GPS*

## Cache Find Log

| | |
|---|---|
| Date | |
| Find Number | |
| Cache Name | |
| Cache GC Code | |
| Latitude | |
| Longitude | |
| Took / Left | |
| Travel Bugs | |
| Notes | |

| | |
|---|---|
| Date | |
| Find Number | |
| Cache Name | |
| Cache GC Code | |
| Latitude | |
| Longitude | |
| Took / Left | |
| Travel Bugs | |
| Notes | |

## Cache Find Log

| | |
|---|---|
| Date | |
| Find Number | |
| Cache Name | |
| Cache GC Code | |
| Latitude | |
| Longitude | |
| Took / Left | |
| Travel Bugs | |
| Notes | |

| | |
|---|---|
| Date | |
| Find Number | |
| Cache Name | |
| Cache GC Code | |
| Latitude | |
| Longitude | |
| Took / Left | |
| Travel Bugs | |
| Notes | |

## Cache Find Log

| | |
|---|---|
| Date | |
| Find Number | |
| Cache Name | |
| Cache GC Code | |
| Latitude | |
| Longitude | |
| Took / Left | |
| Travel Bugs | |
| Notes | |

| | |
|---|---|
| Date | |
| Find Number | |
| Cache Name | |
| Cache GC Code | |
| Latitude | |
| Longitude | |
| Took / Left | |
| Travel Bugs | |
| Notes | |

www.GeocachingClassroom.com

## Cache Find Log

| | |
|---|---|
| Date | |
| Find Number | |
| Cache Name | |
| Cache GC Code | |
| Latitude | |
| Longitude | |
| Took / Left | |
| Travel Bugs | |
| Notes | |

| | |
|---|---|
| Date | |
| Find Number | |
| Cache Name | |
| Cache GC Code | |
| Latitude | |
| Longitude | |
| Took / Left | |
| Travel Bugs | |
| Notes | |

## Cache Find Log

| | |
|---|---|
| Date | |
| Find Number | |
| Cache Name | |
| Cache GC Code | |
| Latitude | |
| Longitude | |
| Took / Left | |
| Travel Bugs | |
| Notes | |

| | |
|---|---|
| Date | |
| Find Number | |
| Cache Name | |
| Cache GC Code | |
| Latitude | |
| Longitude | |
| Took / Left | |
| Travel Bugs | |
| Notes | |

*www.GeocachingClassroom.com*

## Cache Find Log

| | |
|---|---|
| Date | |
| Find Number | |
| Cache Name | |
| Cache GC Code | |
| Latitude | |
| Longitude | |
| Took / Left | |
| Travel Bugs | |
| Notes | |

| | |
|---|---|
| Date | |
| Find Number | |
| Cache Name | |
| Cache GC Code | |
| Latitude | |
| Longitude | |
| Took / Left | |
| Travel Bugs | |
| Notes | |

## Cache Find Log

| | |
|---|---|
| Date | |
| Find Number | |
| Cache Name | |
| Cache GC Code | |
| Latitude | |
| Longitude | |
| Took / Left | |
| Travel Bugs | |
| Notes | |

| | |
|---|---|
| Date | |
| Find Number | |
| Cache Name | |
| Cache GC Code | |
| Latitude | |
| Longitude | |
| Took / Left | |
| Travel Bugs | |
| Notes | |

*www.GeocachingClassroom.com*

# Cache Find Log

| | |
|---|---|
| Date | |
| Find Number | |
| Cache Name | |
| Cache GC Code | |
| Latitude | |
| Longitude | |
| Took / Left | |
| Travel Bugs | |
| Notes | |

| | |
|---|---|
| Date | |
| Find Number | |
| Cache Name | |
| Cache GC Code | |
| Latitude | |
| Longitude | |
| Took / Left | |
| Travel Bugs | |
| Notes | |

## Cache Find Log

| | |
|---|---|
| Date | |
| Find Number | |
| Cache Name | |
| Cache GC Code | |
| Latitude | |
| Longitude | |
| Took / Left | |
| Travel Bugs | |
| Notes | |

| | |
|---|---|
| Date | |
| Find Number | |
| Cache Name | |
| Cache GC Code | |
| Latitude | |
| Longitude | |
| Took / Left | |
| Travel Bugs | |
| Notes | |

www.GeocachingClassroom.com

## Cache Find Log

| | |
|---|---|
| Date | |
| Find Number | |
| Cache Name | |
| Cache GC Code | |
| Latitude | |
| Longitude | |
| Took / Left | |
| Travel Bugs | |
| Notes | |

| | |
|---|---|
| Date | |
| Find Number | |
| Cache Name | |
| Cache GC Code | |
| Latitude | |
| Longitude | |
| Took / Left | |
| Travel Bugs | |
| Notes | |

*Geocaching with a Garmin GPS*

## Cache Find Log

| | |
|---|---|
| Date | |
| Find Number | |
| Cache Name | |
| Cache GC Code | |
| Latitude | |
| Longitude | |
| Took / Left | |
| Travel Bugs | |
| Notes | |

| | |
|---|---|
| Date | |
| Find Number | |
| Cache Name | |
| Cache GC Code | |
| Latitude | |
| Longitude | |
| Took / Left | |
| Travel Bugs | |
| Notes | |

## Cache Find Log

| | |
|---|---|
| Date | |
| Find Number | |
| Cache Name | |
| Cache GC Code | |
| Latitude | |
| Longitude | |
| Took / Left | |
| Travel Bugs | |
| Notes | |

| | |
|---|---|
| Date | |
| Find Number | |
| Cache Name | |
| Cache GC Code | |
| Latitude | |
| Longitude | |
| Took / Left | |
| Travel Bugs | |
| Notes | |

## Cache Find Log

| Date | |
|---|---|
| Find Number | |
| Cache Name | |
| Cache GC Code | |
| Latitude | |
| Longitude | |
| Took / Left | |
| Travel Bugs | |
| Notes | |

| Date | |
|---|---|
| Find Number | |
| Cache Name | |
| Cache GC Code | |
| Latitude | |
| Longitude | |
| Took / Left | |
| Travel Bugs | |
| Notes | |

## Cache Find Log

| Date | |
|---|---|
| Find Number | |
| Cache Name | |
| Cache GC Code | |
| Latitude | |
| Longitude | |
| Took / Left | |
| Travel Bugs | |
| Notes | |

| Date | |
|---|---|
| Find Number | |
| Cache Name | |
| Cache GC Code | |
| Latitude | |
| Longitude | |
| Took / Left | |
| Travel Bugs | |
| Notes | |

*Geocaching with a Garmin GPS*

## Cache Find Log

| | |
|---|---|
| Date | |
| Find Number | |
| Cache Name | |
| Cache GC Code | |
| Latitude | |
| Longitude | |
| Took / Left | |
| Travel Bugs | |
| Notes | |

| | |
|---|---|
| Date | |
| Find Number | |
| Cache Name | |
| Cache GC Code | |
| Latitude | |
| Longitude | |
| Took / Left | |
| Travel Bugs | |
| Notes | |

www.GeocachingClassroom.com

## Cache Find Log

| | |
|---|---|
| Date | |
| Find Number | |
| Cache Name | |
| Cache GC Code | |
| Latitude | |
| Longitude | |
| Took / Left | |
| Travel Bugs | |
| Notes | |

| | |
|---|---|
| Date | |
| Find Number | |
| Cache Name | |
| Cache GC Code | |
| Latitude | |
| Longitude | |
| Took / Left | |
| Travel Bugs | |
| Notes | |

*Geocaching with a Garmin GPS*

## Cache Find Log

| | |
|---|---|
| Date | |
| Find Number | |
| Cache Name | |
| Cache GC Code | |
| Latitude | |
| Longitude | |
| Took / Left | |
| Travel Bugs | |
| Notes | |

| | |
|---|---|
| Date | |
| Find Number | |
| Cache Name | |
| Cache GC Code | |
| Latitude | |
| Longitude | |
| Took / Left | |
| Travel Bugs | |
| Notes | |

# Cache Find Log

| | |
|---|---|
| Date | |
| Find Number | |
| Cache Name | |
| Cache GC Code | |
| Latitude | |
| Longitude | |
| Took / Left | |
| Travel Bugs | |
| Notes | |

| | |
|---|---|
| Date | |
| Find Number | |
| Cache Name | |
| Cache GC Code | |
| Latitude | |
| Longitude | |
| Took / Left | |
| Travel Bugs | |
| Notes | |

## Cache Find Log

| | |
|---|---|
| Date | |
| Find Number | |
| Cache Name | |
| Cache GC Code | |
| Latitude | |
| Longitude | |
| Took / Left | |
| Travel Bugs | |
| Notes | |

| | |
|---|---|
| Date | |
| Find Number | |
| Cache Name | |
| Cache GC Code | |
| Latitude | |
| Longitude | |
| Took / Left | |
| Travel Bugs | |
| Notes | |